L E S S O N S

O F A

L I P S T I C K

Q U E E N

LESSONS

OF A

LIPSTICK

QUEEN

Finding and Developing
the Great Idea That Can
Change Your Life

POPPY KING

ATRIA PAPERBACK

New York • London • Toronto • Sydney

PAPERBACK

A Division of Simon & Schuster, Inc.
1230 Avenue of the Americas
New York, NY 10020

First Atria Paperback edition May 2009

ATRIA PAPERBACK and colophon are trademarks of
Simon & Schuster, Inc.

For information about special discounts for bulk purchases,
please contact Simon & Schuster Special Sales at
1-866-506-1949 or business@simonandschuster.com.

The Simon & Schuster Speakers Bureau can bring authors
to your live event. For more information, or to book an event,
contact the Simon & Schuster Speakers Bureau at
1-866-248-3049 or visit our website at www.simonspeakers.com.

Designed by Dana Sloan

Manufactured in the United States of America

10 9 8 7 6 5 4 3 2 1

The Library of Congress has cataloged the hardcover edition as
follows:

King, Poppy.
    Lessons of a lipstick queen : finding and developing the great
idea that can change your life / by Poppy King.
        p. cm.
    1. New business enterprises. 2. Entrepreneurship. I. Title.

    HD62.5.K546 2008
    658.1'1—dc22

                                              2007043406

ISBN-13: 978-0-7432-9957-2

ISBN-13: 978-0-7432-9958-9 (pbk)

This book is dedicated to YOU.

CONTENTS

Dear Reader,

Ever since I started my lipstick business at the age of eighteen I have been asked one question in particular, again and again — "How in the world did you do it?"

I love watching people's expressions as I tell them the answer. What began as almost a throwaway idea — "I wish I could bring out my own line of lipsticks" — developed into my career, my life, and my guiding passion. And as people listen to me explain how I accomplished this, I see them suddenly realize that they too could do the same.

In *Lessons of a Lipstick Queen* I have taken everything that I have learned and plotted it out to show you how you, too, have what it takes. You can find, explore, and make any idea happen. The trick is actually pretty simple — good planning mixed with self-belief. And it doesn't matter at all if you don't think you have either ability now. By the end of the book, I promise, you will have both. My goal is to help you unlock the inner entrepreneur that exists in all of us, whether you want to start something new like I did, or just become better at what you are already doing.

Yours truly,
Poppy King

I

YOU ALREADY

HAVE IDEAS

HAVE YOU EVER daydreamed?

Have you ever thought about doing something different?

Have you ever thought "If only . . ." or "I wish . . ."?

I am sure you have. We all have. Most of us just aren't conscious that we're doing it. Nor are we aware that some genuinely good ideas are lurking within these throwaway thoughts.

Anyone who has seen an idea through to a reality has started right where you are—just by thinking about it. That is exactly how I began my lipstick business. Who would have imagined that a multimillion-dollar company could spring from what seemed like the small and insignificant thoughts of a schoolgirl?

LESSON 1: **Everyone has ideas**

In cartoons, when characters have ideas, lightbulbs appear above their heads. Eureka! This is how we think ideas should come to us. Like bolts of lightning — sudden . . . clear . . . visible.

In real life, most ideas are much hazier. They ebb and flow like flotsam and jetsam, bobbing around on our stream of consciousness. And just like the junk floating around on the water, some of it floats away and some floats back. We often treat these thoughts like garbage, but they aren't.

Many people will swear up and down that they are not good at coming up with ideas, when what they're really lacking is confidence: the confidence to believe that their own ideas could be real.

Very few of us experience what we've been taught to think of as the "big ideas" that arrive as an epiphany and call us to immediate action. Yet all of us, every single one of us, experience the other variety: the slow, steadier, repetitive thoughts that seem insignificant. We may be reluctant to call them ideas. We may think of them more as background noise. Even at this moment, you may still be thinking, I don't have any real ideas. But if you remove some of the mystique and realize that ideas don't have to be grand to be bona fide, you'll quickly see that you have just as many ideas as the next person.

There is one simple understanding that allows many people to become successful: Instead of raising the bar as to what constitutes a good idea, they lower it. They realize that ideas are not one in a million, but a dime a dozen. Everyone is forming ideas every day. That means you, too. In fact, you probably already had and acted out at least five in the last few hours:

- What to have for breakfast
- What to wear
- How to get to work
- What to do first once you get there
- What to have for lunch

It may not sound like much, yet the very same process that got you through these basics can help you achieve so much more. But first you need to realize that all the greatest ideas—even those that have changed the world as we know it, the ones that are admired and revered for centuries—were developed using the same neurons we use to decide what to have for breakfast.

EVERYTHING COUNTS

Like I keep saying, we all have ideas, all the time. That means you, too! Still don't believe me? Get your confidence boost right here by writing down all the ideas you've had in the last three hours.

Don't worry if you haven't come up with an alternative fuel to solve the world's energy crisis. Every little idea counts—from choosing to buy one thing over another and why to taking the bus instead of driving to work. So go ahead and jot them down in a notebook.

I promise you, you do have ideas. Perhaps nine out of ten of them are not worth pursuing. But perhaps, just perhaps, one is.

That one could change your life . . . One changed mine.

My Story

The idea to create my own brand of lipsticks didn't come to me in a flash. My process was much, much slower and nowhere near as clear.

It all started when I was about fifteen, when every Saturday night my best friend Sarah and I would get dressed up to go out (usually to some place that involved fake ID). As you can imagine, the process always involved makeup—and lots of it. It was the mideighties, after all. We're talking electric colors, shoulder pads, stirrup pants, and very big hair. With her tan skin, corkscrew curls, athletic physique, and cute little cherub nose, Sarah pulled off the look without a hitch.

Unfortunately, I can't say the same for me.

At the time I was five foot nothing, flat as a tack, pale, and bushy-haired with a European Jewish profile. I have never looked modern and have always looked more like something out of a black-and-white movie. Of course, I felt perfectly awful every Saturday night as I frantically attempted to shoehorn myself into the fashion of the day. Despite my best efforts, I could see that the whole look wasn't working. Particularly the makeup. I couldn't put my finger on exactly what was wrong, but I could see that Sarah looked good and I didn't.

Believe it or not, this murky pond of teenage insecurity was the beginning of what would become the idea to start my own lipstick brand. As you can see for yourself, it did not come in a white flash but was hidden within a tangle of yearning, frustration, wishful thinking, and daydreaming.

It may be strange to consider such thoughts ideas because they don't look as glossy, glamorous, and exciting as you would expect. But then again, would you expect a caterpillar to turn into a butterfly if you hadn't been told it would? Everything starts out somewhere, and I suggest you start out by knowing that your own squiggly, wriggly little thoughts are the basis of what can transform into real, life-changing, destiny-making ideas.

THOUGHT COLLECTOR

Even the greatest idea can usually be traced back to meager beginnings. One person's passing thought or dismissed observation is another person's windfall. The difference lies in whether or not you pay enough attention to yourself to understand that even your most boring, everyday thoughts can be regular gold mines when it comes to ideas.

The best way to start paying attention to your thoughts is to keep a journal. You don't have to make a lifelong commitment. Do it for a week. Keep a log of all the activities you do, products you bought or didn't buy, people you liked or didn't like, places you went to, experiences you had, and observations you made. While you're writing, make sure to pay special attention to the experiences and events that make you feel:

- Excited
- Inspired
- Frustrated
- Disappointed
- Any emotion out of the ordinary

As you're about to see, any emotional reaction can provoke a thought that begins with "I wish"—and that can be the start of something truly big.

LESSON 2: Take very seriously any sentence starting with "I wish"

As we grow up, wishing becomes less acceptable. While we are still offered the token gesture when we blow out our birthday candles, we are no longer encouraged to spend much time on wishing. But while many of us may see wishful thinking as silly or even childish, this mind-set is actually the best place to look for ideas.

To start plundering your wishes for treasure, put aside everything you may have heard about wishing being a waste of time, and go back to the days when you took sentences starting with "I wish" very seriously. If you resist the urge to judge your wishes before they've even had time to formulate, you'll probably find that one of them is the beginning of an idea.

Despite what you may be thinking, wishing is serious business. Some of the biggest, most successful companies in the world have been founded on a wish. At one point, a young Bill Gates may have wished for a better way to access information. Of course, Microsoft couldn't have become what it is today by wishing alone—but the starting point would have had to come in wish form.

Just look at the Microsoft mission statement as it is written on their Web site: "Our mission is to enable people and businesses throughout the world to realize their full potential." This is the mission statement that drives a huge company. Replace the words "our mission is" with "I wish" and you can see that even the biggest ideas can come after these two little words. "I wish to enable people and businesses throughout the world to realize their full potential." Sounds pretty unsophisticated, but the company that runs on it is very sophisticated. And if that doesn't convince you, then remember something I once heard. It is the people crazy enough to believe they can change the world who actually do.

FINDING YOUR WISHBONE

To look for ideas, just plunge into your wishful thinking with no outside interference. Let your mind go completely. And, while you're at it, don't forget the cardinal rule of wishful thinking: There are no rules.

Begin by thinking of every possible ending for the sentence "I wish . . ." It doesn't have to be positive things or noble things like "I wish for world peace." It can be anything at all—from starting a business to impressing your boss to changing careers to improving your artwork. Your wishful thinking can even start out in the negative by looking at things you hate. For example: "I hate cleaning the toilet. I wish there was a different way to . . ." Bingo. The end of that sentence could be your next idea.

Don't worry if some of your wishes are embarrassing or about what your friends and colleagues would think. Remove your inhibitions entirely. After all, no one needs to know where your idea began. In my case, my lipstick business started because I wished I could look as pretty as my friend Sarah. Hardly a Nobel Prize pursuit in the making!

Keeping all this in mind, go ahead and start jotting down ideas for how to end the sentence that starts with "I wish . . ."

Or, if you'd rather, try ending the sentence that starts with "I hate when . . ."

Take some time and think further about things that you might wish for. They could be a service, a skill, a product, an event, a book, a new dance, or just a new outlook. It doesn't matter what you wish for; it only matters that you take these thoughts seriously enough to examine them.

My Story

In my teens, one of my favorite time-wasting habits was watching TV. I loved *M*A*S*H, Family Ties, 21 Jump Street,* MTV, and old Hollywood movies. One of the reasons I loved these movies was the women — Lauren Bacall, Greta Garbo, Marlene Dietrich. Now theirs was a glamour I could relate to. The pale skin, the old-fashioned finger waves, the smoky eyes, and the deep, deep matte lipstick all seemed so much more up my alley than the Debbie Gibson fuchsia lip gloss specials that worked for my best friend.

It took a couple of years and countless makeup offenses, but by the time I was in my last year of high school, I had finally become conscious of my desire to emulate this old Hollywood look. While I could get the smoky eyeliners, mascara, and rouge readily enough, those matte lipsticks were nowhere to be found.

My "wish consciousness" started out in the same way it does for any Joe Blow on the other side of an industry. I had all the same doubts as any other civilian who wishes for something that they can't find. You assume it must exist. You couldn't be the only one who wants it. The big companies have everything covered, right? Who are you to notice something new? Surely people trained in this area are on to it.

So I just kept looking in department stores, drugstores, even at theatrical makeup suppliers. I don't know whether it was boredom, vanity, or inspiration, but by the time I had actually completed high school, I was taking my "wish" pretty seriously. It had stopped being just about me and had become a general question: Do matte lipsticks even exist anymore?

This is where my curiosity really kicked in and took my wish to the next level. I started going out of my way to ask about matte lipsticks, seeking out any stores that sold personal care products, asking other women if they had found any lipsticks that were less glossy than the standard variety, getting tips and tricks to make my lipstick look matte, and looking up every makeup outlet in the phone book. I was still quite some distance from deciding to start my own brand. I was just at the very beginning, at the point where I was conscious that my "wish" thought was interesting and I was curious enough to explore it further and nothing more than that.

"I wish" thoughts aren't always about a particular type of product like mine was. They are about anything you can think of:

- I wish there was a bookstore in my neighborhood.
- I wish there was a home hairdressing service.
- I wish I could bake muffins.
- I wish there was an espresso machine in my car.
- I wish I had different types of textbooks at school.
- I wish my boss gave me more responsibility.

It's wishes like these that are at the core of ideas—ideas that are pathways to a different life.

LESSON 3: You make the difference

Edison, Newton . . . both famous inventors who changed the world for good. But guess what? You can relax. Your ideas don't have to be groundbreaking, don't even have to be new, and certainly don't have to come in an instant. In fact, many of the greatest ideas came about over long and arduous periods of trial, error, and the layering of new ideas onto those that came before. Even Sir Isaac Newton had to give credit to his predecessors, saying, "If I have seen farther, it is by standing on the shoulders of giants."

For an idea to be yours, you don't have to invent something new. You just have to think about it in a new way, *your* way. After all, while I may not have invented lipsticks, there's no denying that I added something to the existing crop. As long as you are adding something that fulfills your own wishes, it becomes your idea. Don't worry too much about how different your idea may be. When it comes to ideas, even a small detail can make a world of difference.

I was flipping through *Time* magazine's article on the most amazing inventions of 2005 and many of them supported what I am telling you—that good ideas are not necessarily groundbreaking. One of my favorites was a new design for prescription drug bottles called ClearRx. Designed by a student at the School of Visual Arts in New York City, the bottle takes the ordinary, round, plastic container and turns it on its head so that it rests on its cap, and also flattens out the bottle (the side profile looks a little like a Popsicle), so that it is no longer cylindrical but flat and wide. This mean the label sits flat and you no longer need to rotate the bottle to read the instructions. Nothing fancy or high tech, just practical, sensible, and user-friendly. From one student's feelings and thoughts came an idea that is now selling throughout Target pharmacies and is considered by *Time* magazine one of the best inventions of 2005. Not bad, eh?

Sounds amazing, but in truth that's exactly what you're

likely to find at the base of many a well-established institution — a personal observation that led to an idea.

My Story

Back when I was scouring department stores and makeup counters all over Australia for any sign of matte lipstick, there were hundreds of lipsticks to choose from. The year was 1989 and we already had all the major brands of the day — Clinique, Lancôme, Estée Lauder, Revlon, Shiseido, and Dior, as well as some homegrown discount cosmetics brands. MAC and a small handful of other indie brands had just started in the United States, but I wasn't aware of them yet.

What I was aware of was that although there were a large number of lipsticks on the market, I couldn't find the kind I wanted. It wasn't just the matte element, either, but other things as well. Why couldn't I get lipsticks to really grip? They felt so slimy! Like they were going to slide right off your mouth the second you put them on. Surely those ones that were around in old Hollywood would have had more of a crayonlike feel.

And another thing. Why did every red I tried go pink? What would happen if you put a touch of brown in a red? Would that stop it going pink? And speaking of browns, you couldn't seem to get one. The choices available fell mainly into pinks, reds, berries, and corals. Where was a strong brown or a true aubergine? And don't even get me started on the smell! Many had such heavy fragrance that it gave me a headache to wear them.

Ever since I was a little girl, I thought lipstick was the most glamorous thing in the whole world. And now here I was, eighteen and ready to wear proper lipstick but unable to find one I was really happy with. I didn't set out to reinvent the lipstick. All I really wanted was a particular type of lipstick — and it just so happened to be slightly different than the others.

Of course, this was all "in my opinion." Then again, that is all an idea needs to be at the beginning. Your opinion. Many of us belittle our own ideas because we believe that only the real revolutionary stuff deserves to be filed under the heading of "idea." But if you are passionate about something, your passion alone could make the idea unique. We're all inspired when we meet someone with a genuine passion for something, whether it be their recipe for oatmeal raisin cookies or their babysitting service. Your approach and delivery can make anything special, unique, new, interesting, and, yes, even revolutionary.

LESSON 4: **Allow for an incubation period**

Once you've found your inner wellspring of ideas, then what?

Well, you sit on them, like a chicken with an egg. This is what I call the incubation period. If you've ever seen chicks hatch, you know about the incubation chamber. The red glow from the heating lamp is so warm and inviting—I suggest you bathe your hatchling idea in this same warm glow. Protect it from harsh or extreme reactions, like deciding it is the best idea in the world or the worst. Just sit on it. Think about it. Bond with it.

Incubation periods also protect your ideas from other people's opinions. Believe me, you will get plenty of those, both solicited and unsolicited, down the line. For now, keep your idea to yourself. Like an egg, an idea is both one of the strongest structures out there and one of the most fragile—they can be tough enough to change the world, but they can also be very vulnerable to outside forces. So, before you go letting any outside forces in, take some time to incubate.

Some of your ideas will survive the incubation, and others won't. Sometimes, you'll find that what seemed right at the start gradually loses its appeal. Other times, you will develop more and more of a bond as the incubation progresses. Remember, you are not figuring out how, when, or why your idea will work. All you're doing now is taking the time to get attached and feel comfortable in the belief that, at the very least, you personally think your idea is a good one.

My Story

My first incubation period lasted about two months.

It was my first year out of school and I was doing a part-time bachelor of arts program, studying subjects like philosophy, psychology, sociology, and astronomy. All very interesting subjects but not leading in any one direction. I was really just biding time until I could figure out what I wanted to do. It was during this period that I started to take the lipstick idea more seriously. Up until now I had just wished for matte lipsticks, thinking it would be a good idea for one of the major brands to put out a line, but I still hadn't made the decision to do it myself.

At this stage, I was just incubating the idea. I thought about it a lot, but I wasn't ready to discuss it with anyone or formalize my exploration. I just wanted to mull it over. As a reaction, I started looking at other girls' lipstick choices, watching anyone who pulled one out of her bag. I would look at women walking down the street and wonder whether they would pick a matte lipstick if given the choice. I started having conversations in my head with some of them. I would ask them if they knew that matte lipstick actually stayed on longer and had more pigment than standard lipsticks. Sounds crazy, but it helped me to really bond with the idea.

Also during this time, some ideas came and went that I didn't bond with. I would get thoughts like, Maybe instead of just matte lipstick, there should be a whole line of forties-style makeup. For a while I would think this was a great idea, but then I would notice that too many concerns got in the way of my getting attached. I didn't want to look like I was going to a costume party dressed as a forties movie star; I wanted to look modern but with just matte lipstick instead. A whole cosmetics line would turn me off because I would see it as too retro. That egg cracked, but I kept sitting on other eggs, and after a while the idea became a part of me.

I still use this method with everything I do. I have given myself a minimum of three days' incubation for anything that I acknowledge as a bona fide idea. Nine times out of ten, those ideas that I think are perfect don't survive my incubation period. But if at the end of the three days I still feel excited about the idea and my excitement outweighs my concerns, then the idea is a keeper.

Speaking of concerns, keep in mind that they will always be there. In fact, the better the idea, the more likely you are to have concerns. But the balance needs to be such that you can still bond with the idea despite your reservations. That is the beauty of this quiet time you spend with your idea—what you end up taking with you is only that which you truly believe.

LESSON 5: **Fantasizing is essential**

To make a change or get something started, a healthy dose of fantasy is essential. While it may be easy to fantasize about that cute guy you just met, fantasizing about your career is a bit more challenging. And when I say fantasy, I mean fantasy with a capital F. This is no time to let reality come butting in on your dreams. Trust me, there will be plenty of opportunity for that later on.

As you try to fantasize about an idea, don't be surprised if barriers keep popping up just like in those car-racing video games where you have to anticipate and avoid any obstacles that may come your way. Except when you're fantasizing about your idea, the speed bumps will look and sound something like this:

- I don't have the expertise.
- Where would I get the financing?
- What about all my other responsibilities?

- Do I really have the ability?
- Who would I contact?

These are all perfectly valid questions — just not for now. Now is about fantasy. So override all your concerns, pretend all your questions are answered, and imagine there is nothing to stop you from achieving your wildest dreams.

These fantasies will help you tap into the passion and strength you will need to forge your own path and overcome your doubts. As you go further, your rational mind will pull up all sorts of worries, and you will need to use backup fantasies to get past these. Picture yourself getting awards, running meetings, doing interviews, having a really hip-looking office — whatever it takes to get you feeling passionate and excited about turning your ideas into reality. Store up these fantasies and keep them in a special place in your heart and mind — they are going to come in very handy.

My Story

My entire entry into cosmetics was one big fantasy. Without all that fantasy at the beginning, it would never have happened.

I had one particular fantasy that I would pull up whenever the idea of starting a matte lipstick brand would begin to seem utterly ridiculous. Let's call it the launch party. I would picture the launch party for

my lipsticks at a trendy restaurant that I was particularly fond of at the time. In my fantasy, there were
throngs of media people congratulating me and lots
of women wiping off their own lipstick to try mine.
I would imagine red velvet decorations and delicious
food, all-red gourmet treats. I even had the music all
figured out. For some reason, the song playing in the
background was always "That's the Way (I Like It)"
by KC and the Sunshine Band. Questionable musical
taste or not, seeing all this in my head really helped.

To this day, I still remember how this fantasy helped
get me through some real emotional low points. One
instance in particular comes to mind. I was sitting at
a tram stop after getting some quotes on letterheads
and business cards from a stationery shop. Most of
my friends at the time were in college with very clear
ideas as to what they wanted from the next few years.
And here I was, in the middle of the day, on my own,
at a tram stop in the middle of nowhere. All of a sudden, I felt overcome with doubt and loneliness. I felt
really stupid sitting there chasing some rainbow of
starting a lipstick brand. What a waste of time. I was
just some foolish kid who didn't even have a driver's
license and had to take public transportation everywhere. How could I pull off something like this?

But then I started thinking about the press launch

and how good it would feel. I got right back into thinking about all the little details that excited me at the launch and how amazing it would be to get to that point. By the time the tram came, I was motivated and back on track. Once again I started feeling that it might be possible.

Fantasies helped me to overcome doubts many, many times and still do. They can do the same for you. Keep that in mind as you work on the next exercise.

LA LA LAND

You've heard about my fantasy; now it's your turn. Forget how, when, even why; just imagine taking your idea all the way to the pinnacle of success. These fantasies are what will allow you to take ownership and become intimate with your idea. It needs to start mingling with your hopes and dreams and intertwining itself into the areas that motivate you. Take your fantasy to the limit. Imagine yourself in the most improbable, incredible, *Ripley's Believe It or Not!* moments. Don't stop yourself in any way. Remember that this idea or any idea could change your entire future. You need your fantasies to set the stage.

Get out a piece of paper and write out your fantasy in as much detail as possible.

LESSON 6: **Ideas are commodities**

Ideas are solid entities in and of themselves. As such, they can be traded, sold, shared, reworked, researched, and so forth. Make no mistake, an idea is a commodity—meaning that when you have one, you have something of value, a value that can be realized in any number of ways.

Once you have recognized, bonded with, and taken ownership of your idea, all sorts of possibilities may present themselves. The one you choose will depend a lot on the nature of your idea. You can develop the idea yourself. You can sell it to someone else. You can partner with a large company. The options go on and on. For example, if your idea is to start a procrastination-busting coaching service for creative professionals, chances are that's something you'll have to develop yourself. Then again, if your idea is for a new flavor of coffee, you could look into doing it yourself or you could approach a company such as Starbucks. Whatever your idea, one thing is for certain: you will have many choices as to the best way to proceed.

Like I said before, your decisions will depend a lot on the nature of your idea, but they will also depend on you and the nature of your dreams. In other words, what do you want out of this?

If you can't answer this question just yet, let your fantasies be your guides. In your fantasies:

- What type of situations did you see yourself in?
- Did your fantasies revolve mainly around people, places, or things?
- Did you keep returning to a fantasy that saw you being the boss and running a staff meeting?
- Did your fantasies involve driving a beautiful car or buying amazing clothes?
- Did your fantasies involve communicating information, like speaking in front of a big crowd that had come to see you?

There is no such thing as a right or wrong fantasy, so feel free to be as self-indulgent as you like. Once you are in touch with your dreams, you will understand what motivates and drives you. And once you understand that, you'll know how to make the best use of your idea.

My Story

I have been "entrepreneurial" ever since I can remember. I put it in quotation marks because at times it was just an excuse to be naughty. For the purposes of this scenario, let's define being entrepreneurial as having a questioning nature that doesn't always accept the status quo and has ideas about how things could change. Sometimes I didn't know when to quit being entrepreneurial. In fact, I actually got expelled from my first

school for being "too different and not fitting in" —
or at least that's what the headmistress told my mom,
word for word. Fortunately, it all worked out for the
best when I ended up at a school that was much more
encouraging of individuality and creativity.

This early experience gave me as many clues as my
fantasies for how to proceed with my lipstick idea.
When I first thought about my idea for matte lipsticks,
I could have gone in a number of directions. I could
have tried to get a job with one of the big brands or
tried to sell them my idea. But while the nature of my
idea would have allowed for either option, my own
nature was pointing me in a different direction — the
direction of the launch party.

My launch party fantasy was proof that working
with a big brand would not be the best way to motivate me. Seeing women trying on the lipsticks was a
major part of my fantasy. This was a great clue about
how motivated I was by the experience of seeing the
customers enjoying the lipsticks. Another key element
of this fantasy was the part that saw me getting con-
gratulated by the press. As arrogant as it may sound,
that part showed me that I didn't want to be anony-
mous; I wanted to be recognized as the person who
had made all this happen. Lastly, my fascination with
what music would be played at the party, what food

would be served, and where it would be told me that creative control of details was very important to me.

Stack up these clues and what does it tell you? I'll tell you what it told me. It told me that I would be most motivated by going it alone because that would cater to my drive for recognition, creative control, and interacting with customers. Had I been repeatedly fantasizing about being part of something big, powerful, and structured, then I may have pursued a different direction with my idea.

As you can see, fantasies do much more than just stimulate the imagination. They also offer insight into who you are and what motivates you—which is precisely what you need to know when figuring out what to do with a good idea.

Like I said at the start, ideas are commodities. You can do with them what you will. But before you make-up your mind, take a look inside and have a good, hard think about your motivations. Sometimes what you'll find may seem selfish and vain. You may be scared to admit that what motivates you is not something that will win a popularity contest—but it doesn't matter. Good or bad, all that matters is that you are honest with yourself about what you want from your idea. Once you've figured out what you want, you'll be motivated to go after it. It's that simple.

Conclusion

I promise you I wasn't an extraordinary eighteen-year-old. I had very little direction and not a great deal of ambition. In fact, I was pretty lost. I had nothing tangible like money or a family business to give me a head start. I did, however, have one huge advantage: I allowed myself to wish for something, identified it as an idea, and took it seriously enough to think more about it. And that's something that any of us can do.

Here's how:

- **Recognize that you have ideas.** When you figure out that your everyday thoughts are often just ideas in disguise, you're much more likely to pay attention to what's going on in your own head.
- **Take very seriously any sentence starting with "I wish."** Every enterprise begins with a wish, the wish to make some sort of change. Giving yourself permission to wish will help you tap into your ideas.
- **Understand that you make the difference.** Your idea doesn't have to be a major breakthrough. Even if the only thing separating you from the competition is the fact that you are more passionate about your product or service than they are, that alone can be the secret ingredient.

- **Allow for an incubation period.** Before you get all excited about your idea and start telling the world, or decide that your idea is too problematic and put it in the discard pile, take a few days to contemplate. Remember, just because the idea seemed great at first doesn't mean that it's the right idea for you. Neither do concerns automatically mean that you should quit. See how you feel after you spend a few days or weeks just mulling it over.

- **Fantasize often.** In the early stages of your idea, it's all too easy to get discouraged and scrap the whole thing altogether. Who needs all this trouble? It's probably not going to work anyway! Sound familiar? Well, this is where your fantasies come into play. They are like a hit of caffeine when you are tired. They give you energy.

- **Treat ideas like the commodities they are.** Ideas are valuable if you know what to do with them. With so many options at your disposal, deciding how to proceed with an idea will depend on what you want. Look at your personality and at the nature of your fantasies to figure out the steps that are right for you.

Even if you don't feel you have any dreams or ideas yet, you can make a start by taking your thoughts more seriously and being more respectful of them. Inside you are the greatest ideas and the greatest barriers. By dismissing our wishes as silly or impossible, we stop ourselves from striving for success before we've even heard a word of criticism. So try not to limit yourself in any way. Give yourself permission to be a wishful thinker and a day-dreamer. Let go of the notion that only big, radical ideas are worthwhile—they don't have to be anything of the sort. And remember, you don't ever have to do anything with your ideas if you don't want to.

We'll talk in the next chapter all about crossing the line between the idea and the decision to do something about it. For now, just know that you do have ideas of your own. And yours and everybody else's are what make this world go round.

2

FROM IDEAS TO

DECISIONS

TO TURN YOUR ideas, fantasies, and dreams into reality, you have to do one very important thing. You have to make a decision. The decision to look into it.

My idea for a lipstick company could easily have gone the way of my other school projects—from my locker to the trash can. Although I have always been good at trying things out, I could very well have done what most people do with their ideas and just let it drift away. Fortunately, I didn't. Instead, I made the decision to explore further. No promises were made. No lifetime commitments were involved. I just decided to have a proper look—nothing more, nothing less.

I ask you to do the same.

My Story

As I mentioned, while I was always a creative kid, I was not particularly ambitious. Only too willing to sacrifice my grades for other pastimes, I had a lot of unfinished school projects and even more pathetic excuses to go with them.

When I was about eight years old, I became the leader of a microsociety using acorns as currency. Every lunchtime, most of the fourth grade gathered in the playground and we set up our wares for the day, all of which you could buy with acorns. We mainly sold skills or stories we had. Some of us sold jokes, others did hair plaiting, and I think tickling was on offer as well as palm reading. It was all very harmonious and democratic.

Nevertheless, the teachers started to get worried about where this was headed and shut us down— especially my booth, where I sold information about where babies came from. Due to the sensitive nature of my subject matter, I was located inside the hedge. I always felt very proud of myself when I peeped out and saw the line of customers waiting to see me.

I didn't give the acorn society much thought until about twelve years later. I was standing behind the counter in a department store in Melbourne, selling my lipsticks. It was approximately eight months since they had first appeared in Melbourne's hip fashion boutiques, and demand had grown so quickly that the logical next step was to launch them in a department store. So there I was, for the very first time, standing all the way in the back of the store, at my own tiny little counter.

That day, the counter seemed even smaller than usual because it was mobbed by at least thirty customers waving twenty-dollar bills at me, pushing and shoving to get to the front of the line to buy a lipstick. I remember this experience as if it were yesterday. It was one of the best days of my life.

I recall trying to ring up a sale on the cash register while leaning down to find a lipstick shade for the next sale. As I turned to take the cash from the customer, I had a real out-of-body moment. As clichéd as it sounds, everything really did go still for a while. It was as if I was viewing myself from another angle and could see the scene of me, Poppy, behind my own counter, selling my own products. A wave of disbelief washed over me. Then pride. Then gratitude.

It was the first time I was conscious that despite my many flaws, I had truly done something special. I had made something happen. No longer was this just some idea rattling around in some kid's head. This was real. I had made a decision to go for it and now here

I was with a line of very real customers waving very real dollars at me. This wasn't the hedge, and those weren't acorns anymore.

Like I said, one little decision could end up making a very big difference. But no matter what the outcome, simply making a decision to investigate your idea gets you away from "would of, could of, should of" regrets and on the road to making your ideas happen.

LESSON 7: Ideas and decisions are different

The process it takes to get an idea is very different than the one it takes to make a decision. Ideas are loose and fluid, not rigid or set in stone. Decisions, on the other hand, need to be much tighter. The buildup to a decision is often long and winding, but the decision itself can be made very quickly with just a small leap over a large psychological line. Once you are on the other side and you have made the decision to pursue, you need never look back.

My Story

I can actually pinpoint the exact moment I made the leap from having an idea about matte lipstick to making the decision to start my own brand.

I had been fantasizing about starting my own company, but still could not accept that there weren't any of
these lipsticks available. So there I was, standing at yet
another cosmetics counter in yet another department
store, asking yet another salesgirl my standard question:

"Excuse me, do you have any matte lipsticks?"

"If I had a dollar for every time someone asked me
that, I would be rich," she said.

And there it was. The impetus that helped me make
up my mind. Right then and there I made the decision to stop the looking and start the starting. That is,
start thinking about this as a real business and, more
important, start thinking about whether or not I could
do it.

Now, not everyone will be lucky enough to get such a
clear sign. Then again, as I was once told, "luck" is actually just a point where preparation meets opportunity. All
sorts of opportunities can cross our paths, but without
enough preparation we may not be able to take advantage of them. I was prepared because I had been taking
my idea seriously, bonding with it through the incubation process and thinking about it. All that was left to do
was make the decision to pursue it myself. That decision
made, my idea ceased being pure fantasy and turned into
a reality that I was ready to explore.

And that is all you need to do: Make the decision to explore. While the idea alone is wonderful, without the decision to look into it, the idea will forever remain a fantasy. Making the decision to explore is not irreversible. Nor is it a commitment to anything or anyone other than you. It is a commitment that says, My ideas are as good as anybody else's and I am going to look into them.

P.S.: I ended up employing that very salesgirl, and she worked with me for about seven years.

THE EARLY BIRD GETS THE WORM

Can you think of any time you heard of a new product or service and thought to yourself, They stole my idea! Maybe you had an outline for a screenplay that you kept meaning to get to, until you saw a trailer for the exact same movie a few years later. Or you may have come up with an entirely new service, and then found that someone else beat you to it.

Right now, just try to think back to all the times this may have happened to you.

Someone out there made a decision to look into their idea. In fact, lots of someones. If you follow their example, the next time someone says "Hey, they stole my idea," they'll be talking about you!

LESSON 8: **Figure out what is driving the decision**

A decision needs drivers to steer it and keep it moving along. Once you decide to follow through on your idea, the first thing you want to do is figure out what is driving that decision. Since any decision is bound to be motivated by a number of forces, isolating the driving force may prove challenging. But if you can clarify what is in the driver's seat, you will be able to avoid wrong turns.

Three main factors tend to influence our decisions. These are:

- **The head:** We can think our way into a decision
- **The heart:** We can feel our way into a decision
- **The ego:** We can also end up in a decision when our egos get all caught up in the pursuit of a certain outcome. The ego wants what it wants—all else be damned.

Looking back at the track records of these three designated decision drivers, it doesn't take a genius to spot which one is the most reckless. As you may have guessed, that would be the ego.

Although I don't believe that regret is a constructive pastime, I have a very hard time not regretting those mistakes that I have made with my ego. You see, even though my head and my heart have been known to steer me off course, I have always managed to become stronger for those mistakes. The same cannot be said for the wrong turns taken by my ego—the only thing I learned from those is that if you take the time to assess the designated driver of your decision early on, you can figure out why you're doing it and decide whether to switch drivers. Or get out of the car.

My Story

My ego has overruled my better judgment on numerous occasions. In fact, it is actually doing so as I write because some of these occasions are just way too embarrassing for me to share in this book. My ego couldn't cope with that! Instead, I have chosen an example that shows what I'm talking about but doesn't send me running for the safety of a witness protection program.

I was interviewing someone for a job at my company, Poppy Industries. The fact that this person was even sitting in my office was a result of an ego-fueled decision. I had met her out and about, thought she was really cool, and because I wanted her to like me, had hinted at the possibility of working together. Well, she hopped onto that casual comment straightaway. Before I knew it, she was on the phone, and then in a flash sitting right in front of me.

Both my head and my heart told me it was not such a good idea to have her come on board. For one thing, I didn't have the first clue as to what she would even do! So just prior to her arrival in my office, I geared up to backpedal. But as she sat down, she seemed so hip and fun. My ego pleaded, Come on, no harm could come of having her work here. Besides, having quirky, cool people around is good for the brand image!

Now any sane person will tell you that wanting to impress someone is no reason to hire them. But that's just what my ego went and did. Needless to say, there were some very real consequences. Since we were never clear on her job description, she was always stepping into areas she had nothing to do with. This upset the others and brought a new negative energy into the head office. I was also often making up things for her to do and then, because I had hired her so she would like me, I had trouble saying no to some of the ideas that these goose chases generated. All in all, it was a bad situation for everyone involved.

Of course, over the years, there were other employees who also didn't work out, but what makes me regret this particular case is that I knew from the beginning that I was making a decision based on questionable motives. And I went ahead and did it anyway.

Our egos go everywhere we go, and we couldn't possibly remove them from the decision making process completely. We can, however, make it our business to be aware when the ego overrides the head and heart — considerably more reliable drivers — and hops behind the wheel. Then we can do everything in our power to wrest the control away from this rogue driver.

LESSON 9: Imagine the worst-case scenario

When you look at a table groaning under the weight of a full Thanksgiving Day feast, you may think, no one can possibly eat all of that! But cut to two hours later and you're looking at a lot fewer leftovers than you anticipated. Risk is a lot like that crammed table. When you first look at it, it seems overwhelming. But if you consume slowly, bit by bit, you can take it on.

To minimize the fear surrounding your risk, it helps to break it up into little pieces. Keep in mind that your goal is to wind up with an accurate sense of the risk you're about to take, not an underestimation or an exaggeration. So ask yourself: What is the worst-case scenario?

The fundamental risk of an idea is always the same: the risk that it won't work. But the consequences of failure will vary according to your nature and the nature of the idea. If your ideas involve life and limb, such as bungee jumping, then the risk of it not working out could be death. In most circumstances, however, while the risk may not be death, it can often seem just as scary.

You'll usually find the following ranking high on your list:

- **Loss of money.** Ideas cost money; if the worst happens, you may lose either your money or someone else's
- **Loss of time.** Time you invest in your idea is time you could have spent elsewhere
- **Loss of pride.** Your sense of yourself as a success can suffer as a result of a failed idea

WHAT'S THE WORST THAT CAN HAPPEN?

For the purposes of this exercise, let's assume that the worse case has happened. Remember we are talking about the worst *possibility*, not what *will* happen but what *could* happen. Go ahead and take some time to sit in this dark place, and with razor-sharp honesty ponder how you would stomach the worst. Here are some questions to get you thinking:

- How do you feel about losing your money or your investor's money?

- Can you think of a contingency plan? If so, what is it?
- Are you okay with losing the time it will take you to get this idea off the ground?
- How would feel about yourself if the worst were to happen?

This is the point at which many people turn away because at first glance, the risk seems too unbearable. But digest it very slowly and what you'll find is that you might be in for a pleasant surprise.

My Story

I'll never forget the first time I consciously considered the dreaded worst-case scenario. After months of formulation, I finally drove out to the factory that was producing my lipsticks to pick up the first order. Seven shades at one thousand lipsticks per shade made for seven thousand lipsticks total. I loaded them into the trunk and backseat of my clunky old sixties vintage Mercedes.

Tooling along on the highway in this tank of a car, I was listening to Madonna on the boom box in the passenger seat. The music is blasting, the sun is shining, and the car is rattling, when out of the blue I become completely petrified. What if this whole thing doesn't work out? I have seven thousand lipsticks in my car . . . What if I can't sell one of them?

All of a sudden, I was gripped by fear, convinced that I had done the wrong thing and was going to fall flat. At that moment all I could see was the worst happening.

For a few miles, I was tortured. Then I started thinking—if the worst happens and this venture doesn't work, I wouldn't be happy about it but I would still be okay. I was going to do everything I could to make it work. But if it didn't, no one was going to die—including me. I started to relax; I even managed to laugh. I thought to myself, You know, it's really not all bad. If it doesn't work out . . . at least I will have a lifetime supply of great lipsticks!

I don't mean to be flippant, but digesting risk becomes easier when you really think about the worst-case scenario and whether you could accept it. Notice I didn't say "like" it, just accept it. Initially, you will feel terror at the thought. But stick with it and you just might find that, come what may, you could accept that worst-case scenario and deal with the consequences.

Sure, you'll still be afraid, but that's only to be expected. Digesting risk does not mean completely eliminating fear— only delusion can do that, and that is the last thing you want at a time like this. It means metabolizing your fear constructively. The metabolic process is the breaking down of substances to produce energy. If we apply this to the fear that comes with taking risks, we realize that we can use that fear to gain energy. A healthy fear of avoiding our worst-case scenario can be broken down and metabolized into the kind of smooth, flowing motivation that will keep us working hard to ensure that the worst case does not happen.

OTHER PEOPLE'S MONEY

Sometimes, in fact quite often, you may not be the only one who would have to weather the worst-case scenario. The risk can trickle down to affect those in your personal and professional life. To digest this additional level of risk, keep in mind the following guidelines:

- **PERSONAL RELATIONSHIPS.** If you have friends, family, or anyone else who relies on you financially or otherwise, you may need to see if they can tolerate the risk you're about to take. If they can't, the risk becomes larger still, which can affect your decision. Should making your family and friends uncomfortable make the risk too much of a burden, you are bound to feel ill at ease. In the next section, we will talk about how to recognize and work through these feelings.

- **PROFESSIONAL RELATIONSHIPS.** While you'd do well to consider the risk tolerance of those who depend on you in your personal life, the same does not hold true in your professional life. If the result of an idea not working out means a loss of time, money, or pride for business partners, professional colleagues, or coworkers, then it's up to them to figure out whether or not they can digest the risk. You do not have to take on their fears. As long as you have been completely honest with the information and are willing to do your part, it is up to them to assess their own ability to handle the worst. If anyone refuses to do this and makes you feel that their risk is your responsibility alone, then that is a sign not to get professionally involved with them. Ideas often involve an inherent risk. One way to minimize the size of the risk is to ensure at the start that any professionals joining with you are willing to take responsibility for their own actions.

LESSON 10: Use instinct to navigate a decision

"Gut instinct": ever wonder where the term comes from? Apparently, our stomach shares neurotransmitters similar to those in our brain, so that our emotions, feelings, and reactions flow directly from our brain to our stomach. What we feel in our gut can sometimes be closer to our instinct than what we reason with our brain.

While our brain can try to convince us to follow a certain path, our gut is what ultimately tells us whether or not that path is right for us. The thing to remember is that everyone is different. Two people can have entirely different gut instincts in response to the same stimulus.

We've all heard the old cliché that says gut instinct will never lead you astray. Well, it isn't as simple as all that. While gut instinct may not tell you the best course or even necessarily the right course, it will tell you the course that you will be the most comfortable with — which is extremely important when embarking upon any venture.

But please don't confuse comfort with ease. There are degrees of comfort. Ease is at the very top and terror is at the bottom. Your gut instinct should land you somewhere in the middle. While fear is a natural part of any challenge and is just nature's way of telling us to proceed with caution, panic ups the ante, warning us of immediate danger. On the flip side, the lack of any fear or jitters is a sign that you're not challenging yourself enough.

Somewhere in the middle is a healthy level of nerves.

My Story

The first time I knew I was using my instinct as a compass was when it came to deciding where my lipsticks would be sold. Lipsticks are sold with other cosmetics

at department stores, drugstores, and apothecaries. At least these were the options when I first set out to sell my line to stores in Melbourne. For some reason, these places just didn't feel right. In fact, I felt panicked at the idea of approaching department stores.

Now this wasn't just your healthy, standard-issue fear of rejection, which everyone has when approaching outside parties. This was a sick feeling. But instead of chalking it up to cold feet and plunging ahead, I realized it was my instinct trying to tell me something. Specifically, that my little lipstick range would get swallowed up in these traditional outlets. When I envisioned it there, it just seemed out of place, uncomfortable, and wrong. Why was that?

While my brain told me that this was where all cosmetics such as face creams, eye shadows, foundations, fragrances, and lipsticks were sold, my instinct resisted. And when I tried to figure out why, I realized that my reluctance was due to the nature of my product. I had designed my lipsticks to be a fashion and glamour item first and a cosmetic second. If I was going to put these little soldiers into battle, their best chance was on the fashion front, not on the cosmetic one.

At that point, I decided to target the hippest clothing stores in the most fashionable areas of Melbourne. Immediately, I felt scared. Since these stores had no

history of selling lipsticks, I was going to have to convince these retailers not only to take the brand but to
take a whole new category. While the prospect of this
challenge made me very nervous, I wasn't nearly as
panicked as I'd been when thinking about department
stores.

Not only did nature provide us with a difference between
fear and panic, it also provided us with some handy sen-
sations to distinguish between the two. Just think about
how you feel before a first date. If you are anything like
me, you may feel anxious, an increased heart rate, and
tingling with adrenaline. People like to call this "butter-
flies in the stomach," but all it really means is that you're
feeling excitement mixed in with a little hope and fear.

In some way, a slight case of nerves is almost fun. Nau-
sea, on the other hand, is not. If you feel genuinely sick
to your stomach, your comfort level has been pushed beyond excitement and hope to a place where you are not
likely to be effective. Your gut instinct would not put you
there. Your gut instinct should put you where you are
most likely to be effective. And that place is different for
everyone.

LESSON 11: **Get savvy about taking advice**

When setting out to do anything new and unfamiliar, you'll naturally want to increase your knowledge by seeking out advice. But if I don't watch myself, I have a tendency to be extreme. I decide that to make up my mind, either I don't need any advice or I need endless amounts. Both approaches can send me careening into walls.

To avoid this I have learned that before I go looking for advice, I need to understand my objective. Specifically, do I need knowledge about *how* something works, or *why* it works, or *if* it even works at all? Regardless of the knowledge I'm trying to get from an adviser, they invariably give me more information than I require. Now, if I am not absolutely clear about why I am there and what I am looking for, then I can end up feeling lost and confused.

This is how I feel when I look under my kitchen sink. Inside, there must be more than a hundred plastic and paper bags. There are now so many that a rebellion has formed. A gang of at least six of them attempt escape every time I open the cupboard door. I have no plan or grand scheme behind why I am keeping them hostage. I just do. Every now and again I ask myself: What is the end goal here? I reason with myself that one day I will need them, they are a good to thing to have around, et

cetera, et cetera. But the truth is, there is no end goal—
they are just sitting there, taking up room and confusing
the heck out of me as to why I keep them.

I am sure I began collecting them with a clear rationale. In fact, if memory serves, I think I started out trying
to save the ones that would be good for storing my knitting yarn. But now, I just automatically shove in every
single bag that crosses my threshold, and as result the
whole mess is so overwhelming that I have made use of
none of them.

Be careful that the same fate does not befall you as
you collect advice. Before you set out, know what you're
looking for. That way you can take what helps and throw
away the rest.

My Story

I had absolutely no idea how the cosmetics business
worked when I first started. In fact, I had no idea how
any business worked. I had just finished my final year
of high school and the closest I had come to business
was a class called Business Math. Too bad I'd been far
too distracted by our teacher's striking resemblance
to Norman Bates to take much notice of anything he
was actually saying.

So when someone offered to put me in touch with a
senior executive of a drugstore chain, which sold large

cosmetics brands such as Revlon, to learn about the brand-retailer relationship, I jumped at the chance.

At our meeting, the executive explained to me how every brand had a representative who interacted with a specific buyer for his store. Each season new products were introduced and training sessions held. He told me about replenishment (a fancy word for ordering product), different types of sales arrangements (such as buying product from the brand outright, or accepting it on consignment), and much more that would prove to be invaluable.

Then, after all this, he decided to offer his "advice" on my plans. In a nutshell, he told me that launching a brand with just lipsticks was not a good idea. Since other brands had full ranges, including blushes, mascaras, eye shadows, and the like, my lipstick-only line was destined to have trouble getting any shelf space.

Coming away from the meeting, I felt more than a little derailed. On the one hand, this guy was obviously very knowledgeable and I had learned a great deal. On the other, I still believed there was a genuine demand for my lipsticks!

After a couple of days of resuscitating my belief in my idea, I realized what I should have known in the first place—that while what he said was true enough, not everything was appropriate for my situation. He was speaking from the perspective of a large retail chain, not the type of specialty boutique I was planning to approach. So I could take what I learned about replenishment and sales terms, but discard the irrelevant information about what it takes to get counter space at a drugstore chain.

Before you begin any new undertaking, you'd do well to get some solid counsel from people who have experience in the field. Just keep in mind that advice is most useful as long as you:

- **Think about what you are looking for and why.** That will lead you to the right person. In the next chapter I will tell you how actually to go about seeking advice.

- **Understand that the advice you seek is going to mirror the source.** Think carefully about whom you approach for advice and try to grasp the perspective they will be coming from.

- **Allow yourself to take what you need and leave the rest.** When it comes down to it, advice is someone else's experience topped with a layer of very personal opinion. It is up to you as to how much of the opinion part you want to keep. Try to avoid my plastic-bag "situation" and don't automatically store it all away.

LESSON 12: **Manage your inner critic**

Speaking of taking up space, I would like to introduce you to someone you may already know. You may have met him when you were attempting new or unfamiliar activities. He usually appears before you start something and then just up and vanishes once you are actually doing it. He is your inner critic, and he pulls up his little director's chair and takes residence just when you are contemplating some new decision. For a little guy he can be awfully distracting.

I am using "he" because despite his pixie-like manner, my inner critic is decidedly male. Yours might look and sound completely different. Mine is extremely mischievous, and not quite as nasty as he is taunting. The big tease revels in telling me that I can't do something. "Who are you kidding?" he says in his signature singsong. "You can't do that!"

Luckily, I have gotten to know him quite well over the years. I've also spoken to many other people about how they handle their inner critic. Today, I am ready to pass on the secrets to managing this strange and persuasive creature, so you can make your decision to go for it without his (or her) interference.

The main thing to remember about this guy is that he never actually does anything — he just comments. He is an armchair critic. A mere spectator. But if you are anything like me, you may be quick to bestow credibility on his devious little voice. When it tells me I can't do something, I just assume that it knows what it's talking about. But that is precisely what this negative voice thrives on—the assumption that you won't challenge it. It will just throw these judgments out not expecting you to throw back. A ping-pong exercise will help you anticipate his comments so you can disarm him completely.

MENTAL PING-PONG

This may sound strange, but next time your inner critic pipes up, picture the two of you playing Ping-Pong. The critic will throw all sorts of balls at you, but instead of letting them hit you on the head, whack them back. Make him explain himself. If the voice tells you something like, "You aren't the right person to do this," ask "Why is that?" Or if it throws out sweeping assumptions such as "It won't work," challenge it with "What if it *does* work?" or hit back with "It may!"

Take some time right now to anticipate your inner critic's worst blows, and come up with a defense strategy for each. Write them down. Not only will this process help you defend against this negative little voice, but it will increase your confidence in your plans.

My Story

It was such a heady time. I was about twenty-one years old and my lipstick range was a big hit. What had once been just a thought—"I am going to try to start my own brand"—was now a working reality. I still marveled every day I walked into my offices and saw a receptionist, sales reps, account execs, and assistants buzzing around—all because of this one idea.

What's more, the actual offices themselves were right out of my teenage fantasies. Located in an alley in Melbourne's central business district, the headquarters of Poppy Industries was located in a converted sheep's wool warehouse. Inside these industrial surroundings were vintage red velvet couches, huge paintings of poppies, animal print rugs, and blonde-wood partitions. As teens, my friend Sarah (remember the one that looked like a head cheerleader?) and I had often discussed how cool it would be to have some hip offices in an old warehouse . . . and now I actually did.

You would think that by this time I would be feeling pretty cocky and immune from self-doubt. But every now and then, my inner critic could still pop up with his very destructive commentary. I can remember one time in particular.

My sales executive and I were sitting at a long, medieval-looking wooden table in our boardroom area, where we were meeting with buyers from an exclusive retail store. We were really hoping that they would want to sell the brand in their store. I was right in the middle of very confidently articulating my vision for the brand when I caught a glimpse of my hands and suddenly realized how childlike they looked. Out of nowhere, I was struck by the thought that these were not the hands of an adult. Very small and slightly pudgy like a child's, my hands also featured the fingernails of a nail biter. Right then and there, it became quite clear to me that my hands did not look in the least bit authoritative or confident.

I was right in the middle of a sentence when my inner critic seized the opportunity to tell me that I was a fraud. I was just a kid playacting and I didn't really know what I was talking about. Surely these people, with their mature, polished, grown-up hands, were going to see right through me. Couldn't they see that I didn't even have the hands of an adult, let alone the ideas of one? The little pixie inside completely rocked my confidence.

For a few sentences, my mouth was moving but my head was listening to this commanding little voice. As I was prone to doing at the time, I assumed the voice was right and that it was only luck that had got me this far. But just as the little guy was about to take over,

I stood up for myself and told him that even if this was the case, I may as well keep on with my presentation. This show of defiance quieted my inner critic long enough for me to finish my talk and convince the buyers to pick up our brand.

The thing about your inner critic is he deals only in extremes. According to him, everything will always end in disaster. Despite the compelling nature of this argument, it does have a weak point. It's called the middle ground. When your inner critic tells you that something isn't going to work, just tell him you are going to try anyway and even if it doesn't turn out perfectly, that doesn't mean it will be a disaster. The less you give in to this know-it-all the less he appears, and the more willing you become to try new things.

LESSON 13: **Face your fear**

I have spent a lot of time trying to run away from those things that scare me, assuming that the farther I get from them, the smaller they will become and the less they will worry me. But I have found the exact opposite to be true. If I can turn around and actually walk toward the fear instead of rush away from it, it begins to diminish in size.

I remember one of the first times I ever drove in Los Angeles. Coming from Australia, I was on the wrong side of the car on the wrong side of the road. It felt very strange — especially at intersections, when I actually found myself looking for oncoming traffic from either side. I was so confused about which way to look, I ended up looking in every direction — even up at the sky!

After a while I figured out that rather than twisting my head around like someone out of *The Exorcist,* all I had to do at each stop sign was look the way that felt the weirdest and the least natural. I had to go against my reflexes to find the right way to look. It was hard at first, but the more I did it, the easier it got. And it can get easier to face your fears as well, particularly when you realize that that's the surest and quickest way to overcome them.

My Story

After six years in business, I was at a point where I needed more financing to grow the company. But the one thing that scared me for years was the thought of becoming reliant on a bank. In an attempt to avoid this scenario, I opted for business partners whose financing solved the short-term issues.

Unfortunately, the mix of skills and personalities that came with these new partnerships didn't help in the long term. Our problems went from bad to worse, and in the end, the very thing I had been most afraid of happened: We had no choice but to get the bank involved. It was one of my worst fears realized.

But what I found was that dealing with the bank wasn't anywhere near as bad as I had imagined. I am not going to say it was fun, because it wasn't, but it was hardly the huge demon I had expected. In fact, the bank actually helped stabilize the business.

Other aspects of the situation were much more painful. And what really hurt the most was that many of these painful consequences had come about as a result of running away from fear and hiding in short-term solutions. Only once when I hit a brick wall, and had no option other than to face down my fear, did I learn that fear is more likely to disappear when it is confronted rather than avoided.

The one thing I can promise you is that fear never goes away. Despite all my successes and can-do attitude, the old anxiety still comes up every time I make a decision to strike out in a new direction. Fortunately, these days, I am much better at walking toward my fears—and it still amazes me to see them grow smaller upon my approach.

Conclusion

People who get ahead may take any number of different routes to success, but they all have one important factor in common: At some point they mustered up their courage and made the decision to explore their ideas. In so doing, they rescued their dreams from that "what if" pile we all tend to pick over in our more contemplative moments, and moved them into the "goal" category.

More than anything else, it is self-doubt that gets in the way of our decisions. Once you get past that, you'll be on the verge of something so much greater than you can ever imagine. To get there, keep in mind the advice in this chapter:

- **Realize that ideas and decisions are different.** Although an idea can take months to form, decisions are made in an instant. Once you decide to explore your idea, it's no longer some nebulous idea that's floating about your mind, but a solid goal to investigate.
- **Figure out what is driving the decision.** You never want to pursue an idea for the wrong reasons. Examine your motivations very carefully. Are they substantial or vain? Rational or emotional? Or both? If you can be honest with yourself and still stay determined to press on, you're on the right path.
- **Imagine the worst-case scenario.** The thought of the risk involved in pursuing an idea can be enough to turn us off the entire enterprise. But that's only because we're unsure of how we would react to the

worst-case scenario. Often, it's just the fear of the
unknown reaction that stops us in our tracks.

- **Use instinct to navigate a decision.** There is a difference between healthy fear and all-out panic. The former lets you know you're on the right track; the latter
  is a signal to run for cover. Listening to your feelings
  will help guide you in the right direction. If something
  feels absolutely terrifying, that usually means that it's
  not right for you. Then again, if it's too easy, maybe
  you aren't pushing yourself hard enough.

- **Get savvy about taking advice.** When you're beginning to pursue an idea, you're going to want to gather insider information from people in the know. But
  bear in mind that you don't need to hold on to every
  piece of advice someone gives you. Just because a
  person is a valuable source doesn't mean they are
  right about everything.

- **Manage your inner critic.** We all have an inner critic,
  that negative little voice in our heads that loves to
  contradict every hopeful, positive thing we dream
  up. Our inner critic's only goal is keep us from trying anything new. You should do everything you
  can to overcome its reservations and silence it long
  enough to get something done.

- **Face your fear.** Like I said before, fear is a healthy
  component of doing something new. It's nature's way

of telling you to proceed with caution—"proceed" being the operative word.

You don't need to go to the same extremes as I did to benefit from the lessons I learned. However, you will have to become decisive if you want to succeed. And to do that, you need only dispel the negative interference, make a decision, and follow your dreams with confidence and clarity.

3

RESEARCH IS SIMPLER
THAN IT SOUNDS

MUCH LIKE YOUR voice, your thoughts have a tone. Just the thought of certain words never fails to fill me with dread. "Personal trainer," "overdue," "credit report" (in fact, "report of any kind"), and "rodents" all spring to mind. At one point, the word "research" was also on my list, but not anymore.

While there are those of us who love the research process, most people will readily admit that they'll only start researching when and if they absolutely have to. In this chapter, you'll see why research is so crucial to any idea you want to pursue, be it a new product or a proposal for your boss.

My Story

In high school, my friends were forever breaking up and making up with me. You see, I wasn't what you would call an easy friend. While I liked a good bitchfest as much as the next girl, I was just as—if not more—likely to drag them into long-winded and highly analytical conversations about the meaning of life. As you can imagine, many of my close friends often decided they needed a break.

But a few years later, these same friends were eager to take part in my questioning ways. Because this time, the questions were all about lipstick.

I had spent a few months traveling back and forth from the lipstick factory and hanging out in their amateur excuse for a lab. Inside were three cosmetics chemists, a few bits of apparatus, lots of bottles filled with various powders and colored pigments, some weighing and measuring implements, an ordinary old stove, and a fridge.

All of this stuff was used to formulate lipstick samples. The chemists would meticulously add and record what they were putting into the mixture, heat it all up, pour it into a lipstick mold, put it in the fridge, then assess the outcome.

That was where I came in.

I would wait for it to cool, then run to the bathroom mirror to try it on. While I was not able to give them technical feedback, I did know what I wanted the lipstick to feel and look like once it was on the lips. So I would go back to them with comments like "It drags too much on application," or "Can you make it feel less powdery?"

Finally, I had what I thought was the right formula. Rich, matte, and crayonlike without being gritty, it was exactly what I wanted. Still, I thought it would be a good idea to get more opinions. That's when I switched into research mode. Suddenly every female I knew became a potential customer, a guinea pig, and a gold mine of valuable information, all wrapped up into one.

I asked all my friends and lipstick-wearing acquaintances to try out the lipstick. And despite this informal approach, I ended up going to market with a much better product thanks to their feedback.

As you can see, research doesn't have to be a dreadful chore. In fact, you'll often find that it can be quite simple and a lot of fun, depending on how you approach it.

LESSON 14: **Avoid overcomplication**

You can put away your Bunsen burner right now, because just like your idea, your research doesn't have to be complicated, scientific, or groundbreaking to be useful. In fact, your biggest challenge may well lie in keeping things simple and becoming confident in the fact that, scientific or not, you already know all about how to conduct research.

Whether or not you own a lab coat, my bet is that you're doing research all the time—often, without even knowing it. For instance, if you've ever organized plans to see a movie, you probably did something like:

1. Decided on the movie you wanted to see
2. Looked up where it was playing
3. Organized with others which cinema made the most sense for all
4. Chose a time
5. Figured out the most convenient way to obtain tickets
6. Estimated the best time to get there and organized a meeting spot

Guess what? That is all research. We do all of the above without even batting an eye, yet the process involves analysis, assessment, and activity. So there you have it:

If you can go see a movie, you already know how to do research.

Of course, you can make going to a movie extremely complicated or extremely simple. For instance, you could read reviews for every movie, plot out a graph of all the critics' opinions, assess each theater's sanitation standards according to a standardized bell curve, evaluate the snack bar offerings against the healthy-diet pyramid, and then estimate the average time it takes to get to the theater divided by the distance from the closest public transportation and multiplied by traffic congestion. Aaarrrgh!

If you had to do all this, you would probably end up deciding just to stay home. But hopefully you can see my point — even researching an idea as simple as going to see a movie can be made complicated or simple.

My Story

Whether I am telling my story at a dinner party or speaking in a fancy hotel ballroom in front of a thousand people, there is one question that seems to intrigue people the most. With eyes as wide as saucers and voices hushed in amazement, they come up to me and ask:

"How did you know how to get lipsticks made?"

"I looked it up in the phone book," I tell them.

Yes, that is right. I sat down cross-legged on the

floor of my mom's living room and looked up "cosmetic manufacturers" in the yellow pages, the same
way I would if I needed to find a floor polishing service. Upon explaining this to people, I would watch
the awe disappear from their faces and be replaced
with a bit of embarrassment when they realized the
very basic answer to what they had assumed must be
such a complex process.

The Cosmetic Manufacturing section in the phone
book had about three full pages of numbers for companies with names like Logipack and Ivreson Manufacturing Co. Not exactly self-explanatory. So I just
started going down the list alphabetically. When
someone answered, I would ask "Do you make lipsticks at your factory?" Being in Australia, the majority of the places I called made sun-care products, but
eventually I hit on a lead. They didn't make lipsticks
themselves but the guy said (and I quote) "I know of a
mob out in Bayswater who are in that game." After a
longish pause he retrieved the name from his memory
and bingo . . . I looked up the number and the rest, as
they say, is history.

In all the years and all the times I have told my story, not
one person has ever guessed that I found in a phone book
a place to make the lipsticks. Not because they are not

smart people, but because they hadn't thought about it in such a simple way. Sometimes it is really, really smart to do what may seem really, really dumb.

Since all you are looking for at this stage are answers to your own questions, the most obvious solutions are often the best. Remember, you'll get no brownie points for increasing the degree of difficulty—if anything, you'll just wind up setting yourself back.

LESSON 15: **The destination determines the journey**

If you've ever organized travel plans, you know that the first thing you need is a firm idea of your destination. When you know where you're going, you can start looking into transportation options and thinking about what accommodations and clothing you will need once you get there. The same principle applies to research: You have to figure out where you want to end up before you can figure out how to get there and stay there.

Lucky for you, in this day and age, you're unlikely to wind up in uncharted territory. Whatever the nature of your idea, someone else is bound to have done something similar. And if they have, then they will have left tracks for you to follow. There is no shame in following these tracks when it comes to your idea. In fact, not only will following in these footsteps help you figure out some of the key steps you need to take, but it will also help you to refine and improve upon the course.

Remember, you are not looking to copy anyone. On the contrary, what you are looking for are clues — clues as to how you could not only get somewhere, but get there better. And like I said, the simplest way to get these clues is to research the destinations where you'd like to end up.

My Story

When it came to plotting out the key steps involved in starting and selling a lipstick brand, I headed straight for my ultimate destination: the department store. But this time, instead of just asking for matte lipsticks I came armed with a clipboard. Now, if you ever feel like you're lacking in purpose, I highly suggest looking into one of these. Just holding it in your hand makes you feel extremely official.

Clipboard in hand, I officially observed the brands and looked for the things they all had in common. After the day was through, my notes looked something like this:

- Display units
- Promotional materials
- Tester products

Now I had a list of things that I knew I needed to investigate.

Figuring out where to find these things would be a whole separate journey, but it was only through observing other brands in my desired destination that I even began to understand what I would need for my own route.

Before you look for the answers, you have to find the right questions. At the beginning of any venture, most of us are faced with something that looks like one huge, overwhelming question mark. Imagine what it must have been like for the early explorers setting out in a world not knowing what to expect. They just had to set sail, cross their fingers, and hope for the best. But you don't have to—not if you look to the example set by the explorers that have come before you.

LESSON 16: Go back to school

As you may have gathered, I was hardly a model student, particularly when it came to homework. It wasn't the assignments themselves but the discipline of actually sitting down to do them that I struggled with. I would observe other students and genuinely marvel at how they managed to complete their homework. How do they do it?

In retrospect, I understand what separated me from these others. Instead of wasting time questioning whether or not they should do their assignments, they accepted them as a fact of life. I finally got the hang of this when I followed up on my lipstick idea and realized that the only secret to doing homework was to actually do it instead of debating it.

Although this realization kicked in six months too late to change my final exam results, it was just in time to help me investigate my idea. With the atmosphere of the schoolroom fresh in my mind, I approached my very adult task with the mind-set of a student. In my mind I treated the investigation process as if it were an assignment. As if my teacher had said to the class, "Your term project is to imagine you are starting a lipstick brand and identify the steps involved." I didn't debate whether or not it was do-able, I just assumed it was and wasted no time or effort questioning the actual premise.

YOUR ASSIGNMENT . . .

Starting up a business may sound foreign and complicated if you've never done it, but we've all done school projects and can use those skills to research our ideas. If you approach your idea like a research paper that's worth half your grade, the whole process will seem a lot less complex.

Take some time right now to put your idea into assignment terms. For instance, if you want to start a pet-sitting service, you could phrase your assignment like this:

"Find evidence to suggest how a dog-walking service will thrive in this area."

Then you can start collecting information on how many dog owners live in your neighborhood, how many of them leave their dogs unattended during the day, and how to get the word out to them about your business. And that, right there, is the beginning of your research.

Your perspective need not be any more sophisticated than that of a high school student who operates under the assumption that the problems they are asked to solve must have solutions. Go ahead and assume the same thing when you're researching various aspects of your idea. That attitude will serve you far better than sitting around wondering whether or not an answer even exists.

My Story

In my final year of high school I took a course called Human Development in Society. It was the postfeminist version of home economics. The thinking girl's version of learning how to become a homemaker. Instead of needlepoint, we learned how to prove a point. We did projects where you came up with a hypothesis and had to gather evidence to support it. Things like, "Children are more likely to be able to share when raised alongside siblings." Then you either looked up studies or ran your own to prove that it was correct.

I loved these projects, especially because they gave me the chance to use the word "hypothesis" — frequently. So you can imagine my excitement when it dawned on me that my lipstick idea contained a real live hypothesis. My hypothesis was:

If matte lipsticks were available, women would buy them.

Armed with my theory, I was ready to go to the library and look for information that could prove or disprove it just like I'd done in school.

Even though this wasn't that long ago, the technology was completely different. The pre-Google world involved such ancient media as microfiche and—even more basic—manual card systems. I started looking up magazine articles, consumer surveys, and other information regarding lipstick. Although I found quite a lot on the subject, the information was not detailed enough to make distinctions between matte, glossy, or glittery lipsticks. It mostly grouped everything together. But it did open me up to the industry vernacular.

I learned phrases such as "wear," "perceived value," and "repeat buy," to name a few. The research gave me a framework and a language to help me understand aspects of the product that I had not known existed. So while I didn't find the information to support my original hypothesis, I did gain a more detailed understanding of the factors that determined the intention to purchase. If this had been one of my Human Development and Society projects, then my next step would have been to find further information by running some surveys myself.

So that's what I did.

Armed with the correct cosmetics jargon (and about thirty dollars in change for the photocopier), I typed up a survey aimed at finding out if women would be willing to buy matte lipstick and what would influence their perceived value of the product and intention to purchase again. I then stood in a university quadrangle at lunchtime asking female students if they would mind filling out this form for my project about lipstick.

Despite the fact that I may have been breaking about fifteen different campus regulations by handing out surveys for private enterprise, I got my results. While they were not overwhelmingly definitive on the matte question, they did greatly increase my understanding of lipstick consumers. The moral of the story? Like a schoolkid, I assumed that the world around me had the information I needed. And it did!

Just as people are surprised when I tell them I found out through the phone book how to get lipsticks made, they are also surprised when I tell them that naïveté was what helped me the most when setting up my venture. I naïvely believed that my questions had answers, so I quit debating and trying to figure out whether my efforts would be fruitful, and just started researching. As it turns out, doubting takes up a lot of energy that could best be put toward learning. I hate to say it . . . but those high school teachers were right!

LESSON 17: Just ask

When I was about twelve, I developed a debilitating pain on the lower right side of my abdomen. It escalated steadily and it wasn't long before my mother arrived to collect me from the school nurse and take me straight to the doctor. He poked and prodded around the area with a furrowed brow and serious expression.

"Okay, Poppy. You can sit up now," he said and looked at me. "I think you have appendicitis."

I didn't miss a beat.

"Do you *think* or do you *know*?" was my immediate response.

Bold, I know, but even at twelve, the fear of surgery well outweighed the fear of confronting an adult professional. When vital bodily organs are *not* involved, however, it's not as easy to muster up the courage to ask a question. Sometimes we are even willing to sacrifice obtaining information because of the discomfort we feel about asking.

A pervasive timidity surrounds the practice of asking questions. Etiquette relegates the asking of questions to certain sanctioned and established circumstances. Taught to raise our hands and wait until we're called on, many of us continue to wait for a green light to let us know it's safe to ask a question. Most people I know overcorrect themselves when it comes to asking questions and err on the side of extreme caution. They are polite to a fault— polite at the expense of satisfying their curiosity and getting what they want.

My Story

One of the best questions I ever asked was, "Can I speak to the cosmetics buyer, please?" I was in a hotel room in New York and on the phone to the head offices of one of the most respected trendsetting stores in the world: Barneys.

This was my first trip to New York since I had started my lipstick brand. The lipsticks had been selling in a small selection of stores in Melbourne for about six months, and they had been doing so well that I decided to head to New York to check out what was happening in cosmetics and get a sense of the international lipstick scene.

Some fashionable person in Australia had suggested I go to Barneys. When I got there I saw why. Barneys was so different from the other department stores. Everything in there was beautifully selected and artfully edited. This was the first store I had seen so far that was the more enchanting for the less it had. Even though it sold many of the same categories as other stores (hosiery, accessories, cosmetics, clothing, etc.), each of these categories was represented by unique products that you couldn't find anywhere else.

I knew right away that this was the store where I wanted my lipsticks to be. But I had been selling in

Australia for only six months; no one had ever heard of me over here; I had no contact, no foot in the door, and no presentation materials to help my pitch. But despite all that, I looked up the number of the head offices, took a deep breath, and dialed.

"Barneys New York," said a receptionist.

"Can I speak to the cosmetics buyer please?"

"Who's calling?"

"Poppy King," I said politely but confidently.

A click, then, "Hollis [the buyer at the time] speaking."

What do you know . . . I got straight through! I wasn't expecting this and suffered a moment of sheer panic before launching into the basic facts.

"Hi. My name is Poppy King and I am here from Australia. I started my own lipstick brand because I couldn't find a lipstick I liked, so I decided when I finished school last year to start my own brand. I love your store and was wondering how I may one day be able to show you my range?"

"OK," she said very simply. "How about tomorrow?"

Well, that meeting is almost Barneys folklore now. One of the other buyers who was there has been quoted as saying, "I was working with the most prestigious cosmetics companies, all bending over backward trying to get into our store. Then in comes some kid from Australia and just blows us away."

I remember the meeting well. All I had to show them were a few lipsticks and my own enthusiasm. These were people used to fancy PowerPoint presentations and schmoozing that bordered on begging. They seemed very nice but pretty quiet throughout the monologue I gave about my brand. I didn't know what to think. I know now that what impressed them so much was that I wasn't just talking the talk. They could tell by my openness, my passion, and my excitement that I lived this. I lived to make a difference with what I did and that appeals more than sophisticated methods ever can.

At the end they said two things.

One said, "We would love to carry your brand and have you and it as part of our new store opening on Madison Avenue." The other looked at me, smiled, and said, "I just have one question . . . What do they feed you down there in Australia to grow nineteen-year-olds like you?"

Most of the information that has helped me to succeed has come from my ability to push myself out of my comfort zone and ask a question. I, too, am pleasantly surprised and thrilled to tell you that people almost always answer.

Furthermore, some of the most useful information comes not from the CEOs or the hard-to-get people at the top but from people on the front line, people like:

- Sales clerks
- Receptionists
- Assistants
- Assistants' assistants
- Even the competition!

What I found is that human beings love to answer questions and are often only too happy to be asked. Take my word: If you frame your question in a polite, approachable manner, you will be amazed at how much information people are willing to give out.

And after all, what is the worst that can happen? Someone refuses to answer. Unless you are asking for something illegal, depraved, or deceitful, you have nothing to lose. If one person says no, you move on to the next. Eventually someone will give you the answer you need.

LESSON 18: Use Your Webs

When I was growing up, the ability to search for information all over the world without ever leaving your desk was the stuff of science fiction novels. Today, it's not only a reality but a major resource in your quest to research your idea.

You can type anything into Google, and within seconds information will appear. I treat Google as I would a very wise friend who has a habit of going off on tangents unless I give them clear instructions. I ask the search engine direct questions like, for example, "What do women want from a lipstick?" That way you can find answers that you may not find if you just typed in "lipstick preferences." The Internet is so wide that every word you use can change the results of your search, so be prepared to try a variety of approaches. In my example, including the word "want" means I am more likely to get back information that is qualitative as opposed to quantitative. You never know under what rock vital information may be hiding.

GOOGLE IT!

If you haven't Googled yet, you're about to find out what you've been missing. Go online and punch in google.com, then start entering different key words that describe your idea. For example, if you want to create a line of high-heeled sneakers, you may type in any of the following and wind up with different results:

- High heeled sneakers
- "High heeled sneakers" (the quotes produce more specific results)
- "Sneaker trends"
- High heeled trainers
- High soled sneakers
- Sneakers that make you look taller
- High heeled runners

Now try it with your idea and keep track of anything that may be helpful.

The same principle applies for the world outside your computer as well. While the Internet's convenience has made many of us a bit reluctant to seek information elsewhere, each one of us has access to our own web of people, or network. When we first examine this net, there may be no one who immediately springs to mind as a resource for our idea. But all of the people in your network have their own networks and so on.

To find links that may help you with your research, look past the surface layer of the people you know. Your friend Tom may be an electrical engineer, but didn't you hear about his uncle who is in the catering business? And while Mary's accounting job may not have anything to do with your idea for a new kind of sneaker, didn't she once tell you about her coworker who left to start her own shoe store? In the end, you're likely to find that the more you open yourself up to the world around you, either via your computer or your contacts, the more opportunities will fly in.

My Story

While I was still researching my lipstick idea, I took a part-time job in a beautiful lingerie store in a trendy area of Melbourne. I had just finished high school and was still living with my mom, so the job was more about expanding my social circle than my finances.

Sure enough, one of the girls who worked with me was very social and was always inviting me to parties. So one Friday evening, we left work and went to her friend's birthday party. When we got there I recog-

nized a girl I'd run into before. I had always noticed
that she wore very bold lipstick and not much other
makeup. This time was no different. She was obviously a person after my own lipstick heart, but I may
never have thought to treat her as a resource had she
not been directly in front of me.

Seeing her now, I realized she would be a good
person to talk to about the lipstick world. So I told
her I had been thinking about creating my own brand.
During our conversation, she suddenly had a thought:
"Why don't you speak to a friend of mine about starting a business? His dad is very successful in business
and he has started some himself." She mentioned his
name and although I knew of him, I would never have
thought to go to him for advice.

This anecdote is a fairy tale and a cautionary tale
in one. Cautionary because I was too close-minded to
follow her suggestion and fairy tale because of how it
ends. In my estimation there was no point in going to
this person for advice because as far as I knew, neither
he nor his family were involved in the cosmetics business. So I never called.

A few weeks later, having just finished cleaning the
floor of the lingerie store, I was leaning on a mop, literally Cinderella style, when the phone rang. It was
this guy. The girl from the party had mentioned my

**lipstick idea to him and he thought it sounded inter-
esting. He said he would be happy to give me some
advice and maybe even invest. After about a month
of meetings, he ended up becoming my business partner — and the unexpected yet crucial link that brought
my whole idea together.**

I was fortunate — what happened to me is very rare. Learn
from my mistake and keep a very open mind when doing
your research. Keep your eyes peeled at all times and follow up on every lead before abandoning it as not useful.
And remember, while I may have been very lucky, luck
would never have found me had I not been doing my research to begin with.

LESSON 19: Watch your priorities

I once had a boyfriend who had the oddest pantry. He
loved to cook, but only gourmet and only for dinner parties. As a result, he would shop according to whatever
exotic dish he was preparing for guests. One night it
could be Moroccan; another night Thai or French. His
cupboards were filled with strange ingredients useful for
specific purposes but impossible to throw together if all
you wanted was something to eat. (Unless, of course,
you had a hankering for uncooked Vietnamese rice paper

spread with olive paste, cooking chocolate, and turmeric. Blech.)

When it comes to food there are certain ingredients that are very interesting but not necessarily useful, and those that are the staples you can't do without. The same with research — the most interesting bits are not always the most necessary. As you conduct your research, you'll no doubt find that some parts are more fun and appealing than others. Now, while it may be tempting to dig into these first, you will find the whole experience much more efficient if you prioritize.

Some priorities are obvious. For example, your idea is you want to be a pediatrician, so you will need to get a medical degree before you can practice (unless, of course, you want to be a pediatrician who goes to jail). Other priorities are not so obvious and actually reveal themselves the further you get into exploring your idea. For example, your idea is to start cooking classes for kids. You might think that your first priority is to find the right space or storefront. While you are out looking for a place with your real estate agent, she might ask you if you have a certain permit or license. Congratulations! You have just given birth to a new priority. It has become clear that before you can even sign a lease on a space, you have to prove you have the permit. Getting that permit then is now your *first* priority, and real estate the second.

So your prioritizing job is twofold. First decide what seems like the most logical order. Anyone can do this! We all had to do it at school when it came to, say, a decision about doing your assignment before going to a party—and we all suffered the consequences if we got this priority wrong. Take the time to look at your idea and figure out what you need to do first. Don't get too hung up on this first list being perfect, because the second part of your prioritizing job is to be aware that once you start acting on this list of priorities, new ones will pop up that may change the order. Your job is to complete a list and then continue to assess and shift, if necessary, the priorities once you start actually exploring them.

NO TIME LIKE THE PRESENT

Information without any understanding of priorities is about as useful as a cupboard filled with ingredients but nothing to actually cook. Go ahead and plot out your priorities right now in the form of a to-do list. Just put down the most obvious things that need to be in place in order for your idea to happen. If you are having trouble figuring out what they are and in what order they should go, then just jot down every aspect you can think of in regard to your idea. From that big list, pick out each aspect and put it in an order. *Remember,* this doesn't have to be "right"; it just has to get you started on one thing first. For example, do you need to find out how to get something made before you can understand how much it will cost? If so, then finding a manufacture for x is your first priority. It is just like doing a crossword puzzle where once you get one word down, it gives you clues to the next word. From this process comes your plan of action.

My Story

When I found my lipstick factory, I just assumed that it was a one-stop shop that would take care of all the pesky production details and let me get on with the

exciting business of exploring my PR strategy. Instead what I found was that this factory made only the actual lipstick, the goop, the stuff you put on your lips. Every other aspect of the final product would have to be made somewhere else.

I now had to find three more factories. One to make the lipstick cases, one to make the outer carton, and one to make the labels. And I had to have all of that done and delivered *before* my lipstick factory could make the lipsticks for me to sell.

Obviously I couldn't go much further until I researched each of these elements. So off I went to visit the case manufacturer recommended to me by my lipstick plant. I had no idea what to expect and was shocked at what I found. The case factory was like something from another time — and I don't mean the future.

It was straight out of the 1950s. On my way in, I wouldn't have been surprised if Ward and June Cleaver appeared to greet me. The secretary shot a somewhat suspicious glance at my eighteen-year-old self from over the top of her glasses and then continued to type, fake fingernails and all, on the bulkiest computer I had ever seen.

Her boss also looked somewhat surprised by my youthful appearance. I half expected him to tell me to run along, but he invited me into his office and showed me the lipstick cases that he made. It seems the decor around the place was not the only thing that was old-fashioned. My choices ranged from "boring" to "granny" to "haven't I seen that in a museum?" I reluctantly chose boring and realized that I now had a new priority: figuring out how to bring a lipstick case into the twentieth century.

My solution became my next priority: graphic art. I was going to have to use decoration to give these cases some much needed oomph. So I moved the finding, meeting, and hiring of a graphic artist up the to-do list. The more I did my research, the more the next steps became clear.

Getting your priorities in order is fundamental to success in so many areas of our lives, but it's only through research that these priorities materialize. Unless you make that extra effort to extrapolate the priorities from the rest, you could find yourself running with your idea only to trip up on the fact that you have missed something crucial.

Conclusion

The more you dismantle the notion that good research requires some type of degree, certificate, or expertise, the easier it will become. Even if collecting information feels unfamiliar at first, have confidence in the fact that you already have all you need to research your idea and figure out how to get it off the ground. No need to go back to school for any additional "research training," no need to bring in a professional research firm. If an eighteen-year-old could do it, so can you.

When you start to view the world through your research lenses, you'll find that it looks very different. All sorts of activities you may have done a hundred times before can be done again, this time in the name of research. Suddenly, everything and everyone is a resource. For instance:

- The waitress at your favorite café may know a lot about produce supply
- That bookstore where you while away the hours reading magazines can now be the spot where you peruse books about writing your own patent
- The Internet you once used to surf aimlessly can now teach you how to incorporate your business

To research properly, you need only be in the right state of mind—the keys to which we just covered in this chapter. They are:

- **Keep it simple.** Before you go any further, you need to overcome any residual fears of research. Research doesn't have to be complicated. In fact, if you do it right, it should be simple and often even quite interesting.

- **Let your destination be your guide.** Envision your final objective: When all is said and done, where do you want your idea to end up? At every mall across the country? Online? Think about it and then go to that space and get acquainted with it. Who is there already, doing what you want to be doing? How are they doing it? How did they get there? Researching the examples of those who have come before you will help you formulate your to-do list.

- **Think like a student.** Think back to your school days. The good students didn't sit around wondering whether or not they should do their homework, or whether or not any of the questions the teachers asked on the test actually had answers. They just did what they were supposed to do, and *ta da*, good grades followed. That's how you should approach researching your idea, with both a "can do" and a "must do" attitude.

- **Ask and you shall receive.** So many of us are afraid to ask questions for fear of being impolite or somehow inappropriate. When it comes to doing research, this fear won't get you or your idea very far. So pluck up your courage and ask away.

- **Use your webs.** Each of us has two very important webs at our disposal: the online Web and the human web. And both are treasure troves of information if you know how to explore them.
- **Watch for emerging priorities.** When you start researching your idea, you will follow the most obvious track. Eventually, however, new and unexpected priorities will pop up. Priorities may not always be the most interesting or exciting aspects of your project, but they are the most vital to its eventual success.

Worst-case scenario? You come against some dead ends or some refusals to your questions. So what? Take my word: any discomfort that results from this will be overshadowed by how empowered you will feel the more you push yourself to search for answers. If nothing else, you will have some good stories to tell—maybe even a joke or two.

I have a joke that came from my research phase. To this day, it never fails to break the ice when I am giving a speech. I tell the audience how in the beginning I was constantly asked by customers and retailers if the lipsticks were tested on animals.

My response:

"That depends on what you think of my friends."

Ba da boom.

4

LOOKING CLOSER

FREE ASSOCIATION. EVER heard of this? It is not a cult, a yoga style, or a special TV offer, but a method of psycho-analysis developed by Sigmund Freud to allow patients to speak freely about anything that may cross their minds so they can get to the root of their problems. Think of this chapter as your idea's chance to lie down on the prover-bial couch and get it all out of its system. Having gathered information about your idea, the time has come to fear-lessly analyze its fundamentals. To truly understand your idea, not only will you have to determine its strengths, but you'll need to shine light into its darkest and furthest reaches to see what dangers may be lurking ahead.

Before you get discouraged, keep in mind that examining the negatives as well as the positives can only help you in the long run. Once we uncover the things that hold us back from achieving our full potential, we can learn how to maneuver around them. Think of this chapter as an adventure — a journey to the center of your idea.

Remember, no idea is perfect. Even the best ones have their flaws. Your idea's success depends entirely on your ability to examine it clearly, honestly, and without bias, and then figure out how to make the most of what you've got.

My Story

Once I started my lipstick brand, everything changed. Within eight months the business turned over more than $1 million. All from just seven shades of lipsticks and $28,000 of start-up costs. Within a year, I bought out my business partner's share and at the age of twenty became the sole owner of a million-dollar brand that I had created. Within two years, turnover reached approximately $4 million and grew to a peak of around $6 million.

By 1995, three years after launching the products, I'd been named Young Australian of the Year in a ceremony hosted by the prime minister, and been profiled by *60 Minutes* (Australia). I was being featured in magazines and newspapers all over the world, and had even been named one of *Time* magazine's Global

Leaders for the New Millennium. People in the street were constantly stopping me for autographs. I drove a BMW, lived in a large apartment, and listened to a Bang & Olufsen stereo—all paid for by money I had made myself! I was flying all over the world to see buyers and meet with press. In fact, I was so widely known in Australia that I was considered general knowledge and included in the Australian version of Trivial Pursuit. It was amazing! Even as I write, I have to remind myself that I am not making all this up, since more than ten years later, I am still in awe of these occurrences.

But for all those incredible highs, there were many hardships as well. In 1998, just three years after these peaks, not only was my business in big trouble, but these troubles were splashed all over the Australian media. When the business got past that difficult time I realized that despite the many changes (good and bad) that my original idea for my own lipstick brand had been through, the underlying advantages and disadvantages had stayed the same. That is, the insides of the idea were the same even though from year to year it looked so different outside.

The moral of the story? To understand the core of an idea, you need to understand where the negatives are as well as the positives. That core will be made up of both, and by understanding them at the beginning, you will be much prepared for the road ahead. The core of an idea very rarely changes despite how many changes occur around it. Know thy core and thy core can always help you to make the best decisions as you go along.

LESSON 20: **The SWOT remains the same**

When my first business partner asked me to take a small-business course at night school, I was way too eager to get going in practice rather than study the *theory* of how to get going. I think I went to two classes before coming to the conclusion that it was all just too square for yours truly. Thank goodness I stuck around long enough to learn about a SWOT analysis.

Think of the SWOT analysis as a closet organizer for the mind, a tool to bring order to a jumble of seemingly random business thoughts. No need to spend anything at the Container Store or Hold Everything to get this process started. The only expense required is the time and energy it takes to sit down with all your information.

SWOT stands for:

- **Strengths.** What about your idea itself makes it strong?
- **Weaknesses.** What aspects of your idea itself weaken it?

- **Opportunities.** What aspects of the world around you will help to promote your idea?
- **Threats.** What external elements risk jeopardizing the success of your idea?

Using each of these concepts, you are going to list every single thing you can think of that pertains to your idea. It is generally suggested that you do a SWOT analysis in a grid form, like this:

Strengths	Weaknesses
Opportunities	Threats

As you can see, there are four spaces to plug in each heading. There are no right or wrong answers under these headings. This is your opinion, and you don't need a business degree to have an opinion. Strengths and weaknesses are the internal aspects of your idea. What is inherent in your idea that makes it strong, and what are the inherent weaknesses, as well? Opportunities and threats are the external elements. What opportunities surround your idea, and what threats put it at risk?

Let's make this really personal. Think of your idea as a romantic prospect. Look at their strengths: What do you like about their personality, their nature? Now apply this type of approach to the idea you are considering. For example, I liked the fact that my matte lipsticks were different from the others. I also liked the fact that they were heavier in texture and stayed on your lips. So underneath strengths, I could put "unique product" and "long-lasting benefits." Now what are your idea's weaknesses? In other words, what concerns you about the nature of your idea? Just like a person, no idea is perfect. There are things that you like and things that worry you. In my case, because of the heavy texture, I worried that some people would find the lipstick a little drying on the lips, and because of the public's unfamiliarity with matte, I was concerned that people wouldn't understand what the product is.

Now for the more outward aspects — the opportunities

and threats. These are not so much about the nature of the idea itself but of the outside influences that can affect its potential and will need some tending to. Returning to the romantic-prospect analogy, what are the things that you hope will happen when you get together, and what are the things that you fear might happen? Using my lipsticks as an example, we had a major opportunity to leverage the uniqueness of the product to build a niche market. A threat was that a bigger competitor could copy the same product.

Despite any fears that this process may bring up, seeing all of these headings laid out on paper will help you assess your idea. In the end, the more you can utilize your strengths and opportunities, and maneuver around your weaknesses and threats, the better chance you will stand of turning your thought into a viable reality.

My Story

Early on in the development of my lipstick idea I came across a magazine ad for something called the Nescafé Big Break awards—a contest that would award $20,000 grants to six winners. To enter, you only had to have a "big idea" and be under twenty-one.

It amuses me to think back to this competition because I entered it before I had done a lot of research. As a result, I was so upbeat and so convinced that my idea was absolutely foolproof that my entry may as well have read, "Matte lipsticks — if you can't see the opportunity, you're stupid!"

Well, it didn't take very long for me to realize that this is not necessarily the best way to inspire confidence in an idea. The more I did my research, the more a SWOT analysis began to form (before I even knew what one was). As the challenges began to emerge, I realized that there is a world of difference between doable and definite. By the time I had to convince the next person of my idea's potential, I was armed with a more realistic perspective that showed I was both very passionate and very aware. It obviously worked because that person ended up becoming my first business partner.

As for the Nescafé competition, I am sure you won't be surprised to learn that I did not win one of the six grants. But there is a nice twist to the story. A few years later, I was asked to be a judge of these very same awards. They must have gathered that by that stage I had grown up enough to view proposals (including my own) with more balance.

A SWOT analysis is a grounding experience. It forces you to deal with both sides of the idea coin. And there are always two sides. Never forget that just as there are strengths and opportunities, there are weaknesses and threats. By now you have made the decision to take your idea seriously enough to do some research. The SWOT helps you to take that information, organize it, and make it most effective. To put it another way, it prepares you and your idea for the next steps involved in getting out there.

LESSON 21: **How to brainstorm**

I am often amazed at how effective brainstorming is given the fact that it sounds like one of those touchy-feely trends that come and go, like the short-lived craze to take down office partitions and have nothing but open space. But brainstorming is different. As new age as it sounds, it's actually a well-established and highly effective tool.

The brainstorming process is designed to start wild and broad, then end up precise and narrow. When you start, the more thoughts you come up with, the better. The SWOT analysis is the perfect place to practice your brainstorming skills so you can add them to your creative and problem-solving arsenal.

YOUR SWOT ANALYSIS

At this point, your SWOT analysis is the perfect opportunity for a brainstorming session. Since this is intended for your eyes only, there is no need to edit your thinking. Aim for quantity. Under each of your headings write down anything and everything you can think of. Nothing is too obvious, or too silly, or too unimportant to write down. Remember, there are no right and wrong answers.

Think of it like spring-cleaning your mind of all the information (rational or otherwise) that you have in your head and placing it all into big piles. Once you have the piles, you can then start to pick through them to see what you want to keep.

My Story

Once I was well and truly past my first SWOT analysis, I continued the brainstorming approach with many other aspects of my lipstick brand. But never more so than when it came time to name each lipstick shade. By this stage I had finalized the lipstick formulas and ended up with seven shades that I thought were hard to find: a clear (not pink) red, a couple of browns, a deep wine, a berry, a burnt red, and a rusty color.

I never much liked the names that were given to

lipsticks in the eighties. As a card-carrying member of Generation X, the generation that was supposed to be more empowered, I felt patronized and a bit offended by such old-fashioned names as "Pink Chiffon Frosted." I believed women were decision makers as well as homemakers, and I wanted to let my customers know that this lipstick was for them whether they were picking up the kids from kindergarten or taking a seat at the boardroom table. Of course, I also realized that this was just lipstick, and I didn't want it to come across as taking itself too seriously.

That's when it occurred to me that seven was interesting as a number, so I started my brainstorm there. What follows is the thought journey it took me on.

First I thought about the seven days of the week and naming each shade after a day. I thought this could be very droll and tongue-in-cheek; it would make lipstick seem like a necessity when we all know it is a luxury. I was almost sold on that until I remembered those kids' days-of-the-week underpants. The idea of those as inspiration was a little creepy. So I kept thinking.

Next my mind took me to the seven wonders of the world. But that was a little too grandiose. I mean, I love lipstick but I draw the line at calling it a wonder of the world. Besides, who would want to buy a lipstick called "Stonehenge"? Then I thought that maybe

I could come up with my own wonders of the world. But everything I thought of was too cheesy. Sure, puppies and sunsets are wonders, but it was all a bit too Hallmark for me. So I kept moving on.

I did get a snicker out of the idea of the seven dwarfs, but in the end "Dopey," "Grumpy," and "Sneezy" just didn't do it for me (although that does describe me at certain times).

When I hit on the seven deadly sins, I thought, "Bingo, this has all the elements I need." It was sexy and funny and completely removed from the "women should be seen and not heard" message sent by the lipstick names of the day. However, it did seem a little negative, even sacrilegious if you didn't realize it was not meant to be taken seriously.

So instead I considered the seven virtues. Aha, I thought, just before recalling that these were kind of boring things like patience, chastity, and abstinence. Not exactly the kind of rousing, emotional, call-to-action words I was dead set on using. So I decided to pull together my own seven words. At the time I was fascinated with *The Fountainhead,* the story of a stubborn yet brilliant architect who refused to conform. Ayn Rand's ideas fed right into my teenage fantasies of all power to the individual. Within its pages I found the seven words I wanted to use. "Ambition." "Courage."

**"Inspiration." "Integrity." "Virtue." "Liberty." "Unity."
Words I could be proud of.**

Like real storms, brainstorms are chaotic but powerful. Brainstorming is most productive when you unleash your mind and leave nothing out. Some of my best ideas came to me not in a single wave but in torrents of thought — the kind of torrents that sweep you up, carry you along, and then drop you off right atop those insights that are found only in the far corners of the brain. So try not to struggle against the force of your thoughts, despite what a mess they seem to be making in your head.

LESSON 22: **Things aren't always how they seem**

As I was finishing high school, the ceiling of the Sistine Chapel got cleaned. A beloved masterpiece, Michelangelo's Sistine Chapel had been the subject of centuries of dialogue among academics. Learned scholars and respected textbooks referred to the somber and dull tones that the master artist used to denote the gravitas of his subject matter. Schoolchildren wrote essays on the symbolic importance of these muted shades. Then the ceiling was cleaned — and the world was shocked to discover vibrant reds, brilliant oranges, and electric yellows. As it turned out, the original colors that Michelangelo used were as bright as poster paint!

I love this story because it goes to show that traditional thinking isn't always right. Nothing should be immune from question — not even information that's been handed down from generation to generation. Although it's tempting to rely on traditional thinking when it comes time to assess the strengths, weaknesses, opportunities, and threats of your idea, if you don't double-check, you may wind up missing out on some important discoveries in the process.

CHALLENGE CONVENTION

While tradition should be respected, it's not always right. Keep that in mind as you go over your SWOT analysis another time. Now that you have brainstormed up a blizzard of information and categorized it according to the four headings of the SWOT analysis, challenge your own thinking by checking for any bright sparks that may be masquerading as dark clouds, and vice versa.

Go through it all again, and just for the fun of it see what it feels like to swap things around. For example, see if something that you originally considered a weakness could become a strength if you looked at it in a different way. Maybe 90 percent or more of your initial allocations are correct, but you never know—that 10 percent can make all the difference.

My Story

Much of what traditional thinking would have classified as a weakness or a threat to my idea, I considered
the opposite. While that isn't to say that my SWOT
analysis didn't have its share of the usual disheartening
challenges (not every tradition can be so handily re-
classified), there were some so-called weaknesses that
I was able to turn on their heads. For instance, people
enjoyed pointing out that I couldn't afford to hire a su-
permodel as the face of the brand—the "traditional"
and accepted formula for marketing cosmetics. But I
decided this could actually be a strength. Anyone can
pay people to advertise their products, but my brand
was much more real and that could be an asset.

Now, anyone can tell that I am no model. But I
am real and, perfect features or not, I decided that
my real story and I were good enough to be strengths
for the brand. Despite my conviction, I remember
feeling pretty crushed during the photo shoot for the
promotional brochure introducing the brand. Just
as we were getting started, the photographer looked
over his camera and said, "You are very brave to use
yourself for this." It was pretty hard to say "cheese"
after that—unless of course it was Swiss, as my self-
confidence was full of holes at that moment.

But I soldiered on despite the inevitable doubts. The photos didn't turn out so great. I'm not sure what the makeup artist was going for with my eyebrows, but I ended up looking like Brooke Shields and Groucho Marx's love child. I remember feeling queasy when it came time to choose one, but I didn't have the budget to do it all again. So I just accepted it for what it was and hoped that my customers would appreciate the gesture regardless of how bad my eyebrows looked.

Everyone would agree that those shots were not the most flattering, but you know what? Once the brand took off, the very same people who told me that not marketing it in a traditional way was a weakness then told me that making the brand so personal was one of the smartest things I ever did.

Although there are cold, hard facts that cannot be disputed, there are also "truths" that are a matter of opinion and a manner of execution. Before you go out into the world with your assessment of your idea and the situation, make sure that you have taken some time to challenge your own notions.

LESSON 23: You're always on a mission

If the SWOT analysis were to have a baby it would be the mission statement—a healthy little sentence that sums up the aim of your idea. A good mission statement has three main components. It:

1. **Is easy to read and understand.** In other words, keep it simple. This is no time for fancy, cryptic prose. On the contrary, the more obvious the better. Take the Walt Disney Company, for example. Its mission statement is "To make people happy." Now, Mickey Mouse could have come up with that.

2. **Clearly sets out the direction you are aiming for.** A mission statement is like a compass that is always pointing the way forward for your idea.

3. **Serves as a point of reference.** Whenever you need to check where you are going or whether you have arrived at the right place, you can check back with your mission statement. This aspect becomes increasingly important the further along you get with your idea. Many of the mistakes that are made in business can happen when you have strayed too far from your mission statement.

To get more of a sense of the mission statement's importance, let's take the example of one of the biggest screwups in corporate history: New Coke. In the 1980s, the Coca-Cola Company got very spooked by the rising popularity of Pepsi. As Pepsi marketed itself as "the choice of a new generation," Coke was beginning to seem like old news. So the Coca-Cola Company decided to come out with so-called New Coke, which had a different taste, to replace the existing product. It was a disaster and was pulled from the shelves within months. From inadequate research to overly reactionary marketing, the many mistakes inherent in this move have made it a much-studied example of what not to do.

If you look closer, you'll find that many of the elements of the New Coke strategy were actually at odds with the company's mission statement: "We exist to create value for our share owners on a long-term basis by building a business that enhances the Coca-Cola Company's trademarks." The clues that showed New Coke to be a wrong move were:

- "Value" is hard to "create" by removing a core product
- "Long-term basis" is not brought about by short-term fixes in the face of competition
- "Building a business" happens when you add to your base rather than completely transform it
- Finally, the biggest, most obvious departure from this mission statement is to take your existing product and send the message to your market that it is no good by completely replacing it; this is not a message that "enhances the Coca-Cola Company"

Everything you do should be true to your mission statement. That is why the language with which you frame
your statement needs to be simple enough to help you
grow your idea, all the while reminding you why you did
it to begin with. Oftentimes, it's the very first reason you
decided to do something that helps you decide what you
should do down the road.

My Story

Keeping things simple is not a skill that comes naturally to me. I have always been prone to layering
messages with as much meaning as possible. When it
comes to mission statements, however, less is decidedly more, so I often needed to push myself to simplify.

I remember having to force myself to put aside my
desire to tell the customer everything I possibly could
when working on my display unit and the accompanying visual. It was imperative that I concentrate only on
what would make the highest impact. Why should the
customer choose my brand over all the other choices?

While I had no problems coming up with the look
of my display, I struggled to find the one phrase that
would sum up my lipstick's purpose. Since this would
be the sentence that would do the heavy lifting, every
word counted. I would have loved to have had something esoteric and intriguing like "Lipstick to be your-

self," but what did that really mean? How does this lipstick help you be yourself? Given that I couldn't actually stand next to each display unit and conduct a lecture series, the message had to be much more obvious. If my lipsticks could tell you why they exist in one sentence or less, what would they say?

So I thought about that and put it down in its most simple form: "It's different. It's matte." Those were the words on the display. At the end of the day, these were the two main reasons I had gone into this business. I wanted a matte lipstick and I wanted the lipstick to look and feel different in every way possible.

At the time, I didn't give that sentence nearly enough credit. Thinking back now, it was a mission statement that could have helped me expand more effectively as the product line evolved. Of the many products that I later put out, the ones that didn't work were the ones that had moved too far away from this simple premise. Not everything I did had to be matte, but it did have to be different from other products because that is why I had developed a brand in the first place. That sentence had done an effective job of convincing customers to give my lipsticks a try, and I should have referred back to it more rather than less as the business grew.

Although it didn't work for everyone.

> In the early days of the brand's success, one of my best male friends plucked up the courage to ask me why on earth I had decided to put "It's different, mate" on my visual. Being an Aussie bloke, he had quite naturally misread the word "matte" as "mate."
>
> Luckily, he was not my target market.

It is so easy to drift away from your original mission. Like when you're swimming in the ocean and it feels like you are staying around the same area, until you look up to find that the undercurrent has pulled you halfway along the beach. Ideas have similar undercurrents—some of the ones that cause the most distance between you and your original idea are complacency, urgency, and acting without questioning. Fortunately, all of these can be avoided from the start with a simple statement that defines your mission and protects the integrity of your plans.

Conclusion

There's a famous motto, attributed to the Jesuits, that says, "Give me the child at the age of seven and I will give you the man." The same principle holds true for your idea—come what may, your idea will not change at its core. Knowing what makes up that core is critical to success. The Coca-Cola Company is still selling beverages, not branching out into gasoline. The Walt Disney Company isn't trying to corner the funeral-home market, and continues to focus its energy on entertainment-related products. And so on.

As you progress toward your goal, don't forget that your idea is only as strong as your ability to examine it clearly and honestly right from the beginning. The following are some of the best ways to do just that:

- **Create a SWOT analysis.** Strengths, weaknesses, opportunities, threats. These four factors will always affect your idea, so keep your eyes peeled to make sure you're using your strengths and opportunities to circumvent your weaknesses and threats.

- **Brainstorm for best results.** Whenever you're feeling blocked, which may happen often, go back to brainstorming. Practice this process often. Pour out all your thoughts, no matter how irrelevant, ridiculous, or uninspired. When you're done, pick the best ideas and move on.

- **Look for hidden opportunities.** It's easy to fall into the trap of convention, take things at face value, and react in knee-jerk fashion. But look deeper and you may find that some weaknesses and threats could very well be strengths and opportunities in hiding.

- **Write a mission statement.** This simple phrase should

be the load-bearing wall that will stand up against the strain of all the changes and shifts that occur as time goes on. Return to it whenever you need to remind yourself why you had your idea in the first place.

Once you've hatched your idea, made the decision to look into it, and then done the necessary research, you have to go to the core of your business proposition and figure out its essential components: What are its inherent strengths? Its weaknesses? Can you turn the weaknesses into strengths? What are the threats? How dangerous are these? What are the opportunities? How can you make the most of them?

Finally, figure out the ultimate purpose of your idea. Before you go any further, make sure this purpose is clear. The more you progress and the more opportunities come your way, the more you will have to keep reminding yourself to serve your primary purpose. As you'll see by my example and many others, there's no use in having your head in the clouds if your feet aren't planted firmly on the ground.

5

THE ROAD MAP

GROWING UP, WE had a lovely cat named Annie. A kind and gentle soul, she had been with my mom longer than I had been alive. I adored her. One day, I was hanging out in front of the TV when I decided that her whiskers were uneven and it was up to me to cut them. So I got out my scissors and started trimming. A little here. A little there. Pretty soon the only thing left was stubble. I had a nagging sense that I had done something mean, but figured that whiskers are just hair and it doesn't hurt us humans to have short hair. It wasn't until my mom came home and saw Annie that I learned the importance of whiskers.

"What's happened to the cat?" my mother said with equal parts anger and astonishment.

"I trimmed her whiskers," I said guiltily.

My mother became very cross.

"Poppy, cats need their whiskers to sense their surroundings and move around properly," she said. "That was an awful thing to do to her."

She was right, of course. And I learned my lesson and never took anything about Annie for granted again. Her whiskers grew back and she lived happily for quite some years after that.

This is a very strange introduction to a chapter on business plans, but I can't help comparing what whiskers do for cats with what well-laid plans do for people with goals. Whether you're laying the groundwork for a new business or a big promotion, every goal and course of action requires some sort of plan. Plans help you to judge your surroundings and figure out how to maneuver so that you have the best chance at achieving your end goal.

Just going up and away is not a plan, no matter how much we want and think we deserve those highs. Instead, a good, solid business plan helps you deal with the highs, lows, and everything in between. By preparing you for the various possibilities, your business plan will ensure that you stay in control of the business—or your job— rather than the other way around.

My Story

My business was reaching new heights and at this very moment so was I — literally. I was on a plane back from yet another exciting media shoot in Sydney and I had just phoned into the office to learn that we had sold over $100,000 in lipsticks last week alone. Best of all, it didn't look like we were anywhere near cruising altitude yet. We were still climbing! I had been upgraded by the ticketing person at the counter and wound up sitting next to one of the most well-known, wealthy, and successful businessmen in Australia.

We talked the whole way back, him from his fifty-something perspective and me from my nineteen-year-old one. I shared with him how I had never expected or even planned for my business to reach this level so quickly. I was literally glowing with the exhilaration of it.

In retrospect, I can see how careful he was being not to burst my bubble while at the same time letting me know that the business would level off at some point — and that now, in the midst of what felt a lot like omnipotence, was the time to focus on vulnerability and to decrease expectations rather than increase them.

When we arrived in Melbourne he gave me a lift into the city. I was in his huge Rolls-Royce, surrounded by

mahogany and leather, when he said something to me
that has stayed with me for more than a decade:

"Never forget this first flush of success, because
nothing will ever feel like it again."

That's when I realized that even this $200,000 car
could never give him the high that half of that amount
had just given me. Because it was my first—and firsts
only happen once.

Getting addicted to highs creates an impossible situation.
The more highs you have, the higher you need to climb to
maintain the same initial thrill. A business plan cuts through
the rush of exhilaration, keeping you grounded so you can
experience a more sober-minded and sustainable buzz.

LESSON 24: Close the information gap

Aside from helping you navigate the highs, lows, and plateaus that the future has in store, your business plan must
also serve as a bridge that spans the information divide
that exists between your idea and the people who can
help it succeed. It is the letter of introduction that explains your idea and its amazing potential to anyone who
may be in a position to help, from the small-business loan
administrator at your local bank to your Uncle Harry
who has a few thousand extra dollars to invest.

A good business plan should help your readers, regardless of their backgrounds, grasp the fundamental aspects of your idea. To do that, keep these three pointers in mind:

1. **Don't be afraid to guesstimate.** Relax. No one expects your business plan to be perfect or exactly right. That's why we have permission to use "guesstimates"—combinations of guesses and estimates. Business plans are made up of these and other equally achievable concepts such as assumptions, trends, forecasts, summaries, and descriptions. But while you don't need to be exact with the facts and figures you present, you should try to be as close as possible. Although no one expects your business to go exactly according to the business plan, the people to whom you will present it are going to hold you within the range of your words. Any vastly misleading information or obvious discrepancies will inevitably be revealed as you go along. Though wiggle room is allowed, dishonesty is not.

2. **Keep it relevant.** Think small amounts of powerful information supported by credible facts. Forget filler—you do not want to waste space with just any bit of information you may have. This will only serve to confuse or turn off your readers.

3. **Do not discount the obvious.** When it comes to business plans, the more obvious the better. Stay away from the flowery esoteric stuff and focus on what is really pertinent. For example, you will not offend anyone by reiterating that half the population is made up of women—as long as you are making the point for a reason, such as to illustrate the size of a potential market.

My Story

I was in Japan for the first time since the Poppy brand launched in their Sephora and Barneys stores. I was working with a Japanese agency that imported a number of hip boutique cosmetics brands, and they needed me to come over and meet with the Japanese press.

The agency was setting up appointments for me with the editors of Japanese fashion magazines, but since very few of the editors spoke much English, my agency provided an "interpreter," a girl whose real job was as sales manager for the agency.

Although I was assured that she had an excellent grasp of English, I had some doubts (not to mention a laughing fit that spread through my entire office) when I received an example of this "excellent English" in a barely intelligible e-mail from her just prior to my visit. Here, read for yourself:

Dear Poppy

How are you?

One of the popular magazine editor asked us whether we have photos that are taken Poppy (The editor desire to have your photos of when you have a 18 years old or so.

The magazine editor wanted to get your photo to run a story and good old your photos. Photos like your smiling face is great! The reason why the magazine want to run your old photos is to make a process (could be your history) how you have been getting beautiful and run. That is why we need snap a shot of yourself.

Could you bring your delicious memory photos with you when you come to Tokyo this time?

"Delicious memory photos"? You have got to be kidding me! Against my better judgment, in a few days, I was sitting with the author of this e-mail and trusting her to translate.

My first two interviews took about three hours each due to all the information I tried to get across and all the time it took the interpreter to translate it. I told the editors how I loved old-fashioned movie stars and that I always felt that women could be strong and powerful, and that I wanted my brand to represent that. I told them that the packaging inspiration had come from Art Deco and was very much influenced by a brand that was popular in London in the seventies called Biba, a store where the Rolling Stones and David Bowie would go just to hang. I went into all the benefits of my lipsticks, the differences in textures, and where the color ideas came from. I told them about future plans and new product ideas. I even shared my observations on the changing ways that women wore makeup and how that reflected the changing roles of women in society at large.

It only took the first two interviews for me to drastically alter my approach.

During all the background and animation that I provided, neither of the editors even picked up a pen to write anything down. They just nodded now and again. It wasn't until the very end when—having listened to everything I had to say—they got their pads ready and asked the question that was uppermost on their minds.

"So you were eighteen when you start business?"

"Yes," I said. They wrote that down, packed up, bowed, and left.

That was all that fascinated them.

Although in most cases you won't be dealing with a language barrier between you and the readers of your business plan, it is best to assume that you are dealing with an information barrier. Your job is to close the gap that exists between your understanding of the idea and somebody else's by providing pertinent information that can be used as stepping-stones to cross the divide.

THE ELEVATOR SPEECH

If you want to become an expert at describing what your business is, practice the elevator speech. Imagine that you're on an elevator with someone in a position to help your business—someone such as Bill Gates, Warren Buffett, or Donald Trump. With less than a minute to explain what your idea is and win their interest, what do you say?

HINT: The key to articulating your idea is to be both straight to the point and enthusiastic.

LESSON 25: **Start with the questions**

Everyone needs to feel comfortable with the business plan. That means you as well as anyone else who is dedicating money and/or time to the enterprise. The only way to get everyone in that comfortable, secure frame of mind is through information. Think of your idea as a potential job candidate and interview it as you would any person who was applying for a job.

Let your idea take a seat and then ask it the following key questions:

1. What are you?
2. Why are you?
3. How do you plan to produce the results?
4. Who do you need?
5. When will you deliver on these promises?
6. What will you cost?

Let's answer these in order:

1. **What are you?** What is your idea? If you created a mission statement in the last chapter, then you will probably find it extremely handy to revisit it now. The principles behind a mission statement apply to this first question. To explain what the idea is, you

need to boil it down to its most vital and compelling ingredients.

2. **Why are you?** Why does your idea exist? What circumstances preceded it? In many cases, your own experience is one of the key reasons that this idea came about. For example, a friend of mine came up with a fabulous idea for a hospital item after a painful postoperative stay. His idea existed because he himself had experienced the need for this product and could see a common problem that this product would solve. To answer this question, your own experiences can be very relevant — as long as you can point to why they will also be relevant to others.

3. **How do you plan to produce results?** How can this idea become a reality? In other words, what steps are involved in establishing and then operating this idea? This is about satisfying the most basic functions of your idea. Think of it like a grocery list of what you need and where you need to get it from. By showing that you have identified, understood, and prepared for the nuts and bolts of the idea, you will prove that both you and the idea are ready and able to start immediately.

4. **Whom do you need?** As in, whom do you need to bring in, sell to, and watch out for as competitors? Clearly, this question has three parts. They are:

- *Whom do you need to work behind the scenes?* This is all about the team. In some cases, you may need to bring in a variety of experts with different skills and backgrounds. In others, you may be it and if you can show that that's all you need, then you're fine. This part is about quality, not quantity.

- *Who is your target market?* This is one of those times when you can use your permission to guesstimate. As long as you have solid, credible statistics and information to back up your estimates, the predictions don't have to be exact, just indicative.

- *Who else is doing it?* Describe who the competition is and what they're doing. Then explain how you plan to create an advantage and differentiate yourself in the marketplace.

You might want to up the enthusiasm to a maximum in the answers to all these "who" questions. This is not a time for modesty, but a time to boast about yourself, your team, your potential market, and your advantages over others.

5. **When will you deliver on these promises?** This is the time for your idea to articulate its strategy. A strategy explains the time frame of what, why, and when you need to do things. At this point many ideas will have to address the topics of marketing and/or sales. Marketing is about building awareness of an idea, and sales are the purchases that will result from this awareness. Both of these have to start somewhere, but you'll find that there is often a lag between the start of the marketing and the start of the sales. As long as that is set out in the plan, the time lag should not pose a problem.

The basic questions to answer here are, What is your idea's starting point and when will it grow? Unless you have a solid sales history with the product in question, you will need to use guesstimates and their close cousins, assumptions. Again, as long as your idea can provide a good rationale for its projections and demonstrate how they're possible, no one expects these predictions to be perfect.

Hopefully, your idea is doing well—it has told you what it is, why it exists, how it can get up and running, whom it needs and who needs it, who else is doing it, and in what time frame it plans to deliver. At this point, you're ready to ask it the 60 million (or hopefully less) dollar question:

6. **What will you cost?** To figure out how much money is needed and how much can be expected back, you'll need to bring out your guesstimate calculator and choose one of the following modes:

- *Conservative/moderate mode:* In this mode, you would use the higher end of estimated costs and the lower end of the anticipated sales to come up with a figure. This will show you how the idea would pan out if spending were higher than expected and sales are lower.

- *Aggressive/optimistic mode:* To arrive at this figure, you'll keep the spending the same as in the conservative mode (things always turn out to cost a little more than you would like, so don't underestimate in this department) but use the higher estimates from the potential sales range. In other words, in this mode, you calculate what will happen when you spend the same money and wind up making more. This is what you hope will happen.

Of course, you will need to understand both scenarios before you can decide which one you feel the most comfortable putting down in the business plan.

PLAY "LET'S BUY OUR OWN ISLAND!"

While you'll either use the aggressive or conservative mode on your business plan, you may find yourself entertaining more "pie in the sky" figures when you're alone. These "let's buy our own island!" calculations are for your eyes only, but they can be extremely motivational all the same, because they show what would happen if sales go through the roof.

The reason I do not recommend that you include these in your plan is because the last thing you want is for people to buy into your idea on the basis of unrealistic or unusual expectations. Still, there's no harm in dreaming of what could happen!

As I said before, the purpose of all the interview questions that you just asked your idea were meant to establish comfort for yourself and others. Once these questions are answered to everyone's satisfaction, you will be prepared to embark upon the work ahead.

My Story

Australia was well and truly in the grip of a recession when I first launched my lipsticks. Unemployment was high, with layoffs and financial squeezes across all business sectors. Banks were tight on loans, the economy was down, and the air was rife with financial gloom and doom. Australia, a country that had been touted as a land of opportunity, suddenly felt as if it had none. It was as depressed as it was depressing.

That's when I came along with my little lipstick brand and what, unbeknownst to me, was about to become the "good news" story of the year.

I had gotten in touch with a few fashion magazines to show them the lipsticks. As a result, the March 1992 issue of Australian *Vogue* ran a paragraph and a tiny photo. Somehow, what would otherwise have been a simple little beauty item got picked up by the mass media in a manner that no one could have predicted.

Apparently, the nightly news needed something positive to say—and I was it! The deep voice of the anchorman would go up a few notches from serious to amused: "And now here's a story of a young girl who couldn't find the lipstick she wanted so she started her own company! Tracy so-and-so will now tell us more about this extraordinary beginning."

Of course this was great for me and the brand. I was invited onto television and radio panels and news programs. I was featured all over the front and business sections of all the newspapers. I did so many interviews in such a broad variety of media that it wasn't just the women who got to know my story, but their husbands as well! Talk about being in the right place at the right time.

I did so many interviews that I wound up answering the same questions over and over again. Since being nineteen years old seemed incongruous with business know-how, one of the most common questions I fielded was, Does your age make it difficult to be taken seriously? I would explain that regardless of age, anyone who wants an idea taken seriously needs to learn how to articulate it and plan it in a manner that is professional. Good ideas can come from any age group.

The next question would inevitably be, Do you find it difficult to be taken seriously on account of your gender? I understand why they would ask a young woman this question if, say, she had started a new brand of shock-absorbing tires for the aviation industry. But in this case it was lipstick. I mean, whom are you going to take more seriously, a middle-aged man starting a lipstick business because he couldn't find the right one, or a young girl?

The questions you address in your business plan are designed to elicit the information that will either demonstrate an idea's competence or its lack thereof. While they may seem fairly obvious and formulaic, if your idea can't answer any of them adequately, then you need to work on it until it can.

LESSON 26: Mapping it out

All of that plotting, planning, and estimating can be very tiring on an idea. Now that you have answers to your big questions and are ready to format your business plan, you and your idea get to relax and indulge in some relatively mindless busywork. Since business plans are set out in a fairly standard way to cut through reader confusion, the only wow factor you need to worry about here is the one that results from presenting your information in the most concise, clear, and professional manner possible.

Instructions on how to format a business plan are readily available online as well as at bookstores and libraries. You'll find everything from downloadable templates (tip: just go to Google and do a search on "business plan templates") to entire books on the subject (e.g., *Business Plans for Dummies*). In the end, however, it's the information you include to support and prove your idea that will make a difference, not the format.

My Story

After about a year in business, it was becoming clear that I could no longer operate on my own skills alone

and needed to call in reinforcements in the form of professionals. So I put together an advisory board of people who were adults, as opposed to me who was still pretty much a teenager; and had more understanding of the operational and planning side of a growing business. There was my brother (who worked with me), two senior accountants from the small firm we used, an advertising executive with a background in large agencies, and occasionally a lawyer or some other professional.

We would meet about once a month to go over the business and try to ascertain what the future held and how to prepare. This was made particularly hard in the beginning for the very joyous reason that the business was skyrocketing in sales. Most of these monthly meetings consisted of a bunch of fairly straight accounting types marveling and scratching their heads in amazement. I, on the other hand, had no prior experience in business, so I was not as shocked by the fact that our sales were growing at the rate of 1,200 percent per month.

With the business feeling more and more like a steam train on which we were aboard, these meetings were intended to keep us as close to the driver's seat as possible so that we could see down the track and plan for the future. For instance, if we anticipated selling this much, then how much did we need in stock? What other products were coming out and when? What sales did we expect from those? How much did we need to buy up front? And so on.

Now that I had all these professionals on board, I was amazed when I constantly found them passing the driver's hat back to me. Their models and methods were of no use without information to plug in—and that information had to come from me. What were my instincts in terms of sales increases when it came to the holiday season? Did I think this was a product that one could buy as a gift? Did women buy different colors at holiday time? I can remember feeling frustrated at having to plod through what seemed like inane questions when we had big business to attend to. But that is just the point: You can't get big without mapping out the very small.

Although "don't sweat the small stuff" may be sage advice in some cases, it doesn't apply to your business plan. When you're putting together your research and information, it's precisely the big stuff that you don't have to sweat. The format, the sections, the requirements, and the templates are all ready and waiting for you to fill in with your stats and figures. Think of it as one less thing to worry about!

LESSON 27: **Prepare for changes**

Here is something I don't get to say very often: "pheno-typic plasticity." Biologists use the term to describe the ability of an organism to adjust its behavior in response to varying conditions. This adaptability is so crucial to the survival of a species that the adjustments that result from changing conditions can be found not just in how the species behaves, but in an actual rearrangement of the organism's genetic structure over time.

A business is no different in that it will have to respond to changing circumstances in order to survive. Sometimes it will have to make only surface adjustments, and other times the actual structure itself will need to adapt. But how can you know what changes are required? The business plan is how.

Because of the high level of attention to detail involved in the business-plan writing process, you will be better able to assess and predict major shifts. One of the most important aspects of this plan is the ability to see the correlation between action and reaction. Anytime something changes, there will be an effect somewhere along the line.

Remember, changes in and of themselves are not a threat as long as their impact is identified as soon as possible. By updating the information in your plan as change happens, you can then plan to maneuver efficiently within the new circumstances. Elasticity—knowing that changes will happen and planning for them—is a vital part of any healthy business plan. A reinforced physical structure is less likely to bend.

My Story

On the first million my business made, there was an operating profit of more than 40 percent—the kind of stuff you dream about but never plan for. Most businesses don't even plan on turning a profit in their first year, let alone a profit of this magnitude. I wish I could credit these results to my incredible business prowess, but in truth I owe it all to the press coverage. Our brand awareness grew so quickly that a large level of sales was achieved while I was still running the business as a cottage industry.

In fact, when we hit a million, the business was still being run out of my home. Instead of a warehouse, I had my bedroom floor, a storage space behind my friend's parents' house, and the backseat of my car. Instead of filing cabinets, I used an old Ping-Pong table to hold piles of stockkeeping records. And for a receptionist, I had hired an answering service to take calls for orders. Most of the articles that wrote about the product included the phone number of this service, and with requests coming in from all over the country, I felt as though I had won a lottery.

I'd spent so little and made so much that I was forced to decide whether to stay in it for the long haul or take the money and run. I couldn't do both because growth would require reinvestment in the business. Now that I was selling in serious department stores and making serious money, the business needed serious structure. Otherwise we wouldn't be able to service our retailers properly, and ultimately our customers would suffer.

Take, for example, my lack of a reliable system to monitor the ingoing and outgoing of stock. Without one, I couldn't really know what stock we had, where it was going, what was left, and when a store needed more. There was also no way to keep track of all the ancillary items such as display units and testers. So before I even had a proper office, we set up a proper warehouse.

We found a location and got shelving and storage space built in. Then, we set up a small office area in one corner, just opposite a big roller door that was open during the day to park the minivan we had now bought to take the lipsticks to stores and dispatch centers. I even hired Richard, my first-ever employee after my brother. A store man, Richard's job was to organize and pack the orders, deliver them to their rightful address, and keep records of inventory going out the door and coming in.

As you can imagine, people, places, products, and processes cost money, so as we started to get more organized, we had to adjust the business plan to accommodate the changes. It was hard watching the profit margin come down from the lofty heights of fantasy to the grounded realm of normalcy. As I said, for every action, there is a reaction. The business plan's reaction was clear in the bottom line—the one that shows what is left after expenses. Fortunately, the changes were also felt in the top line—the one that tracks sales volume. Because we were spending more, we were equipped to service new stores and accounts—and that translated into more sales, customers, and ultimately more money.

Every detail of the business plan has its own ripple effect. Some of these ripples will be large and far-reaching, while others will affect only the smallest surface area near the point of impact. The wonderful thing about a business plan is that it allows you to clearly see and understand the effects of your business decisions.

Conclusion

One of my favorite fairy tales is *The Wizard of Oz,* which tells us that we often possess skills we don't realize we have until we are pushed to find them. The business plan can be a lot like this. Many of us assume it is beyond our expertise, but all you really need is the courage to give it a try, the willingness to put your brain into the details, and the heart to follow your dreams by following a plan.

Writing a business plan can feel like a frightening proposition, but once you get started, you'll find that there is no wizardry behind it, just good old-fashioned planning and hard work—which will hopefully be made easier by these lessons we just covered in this chapter:

- **Close the information gap.** Keep the purpose of the business plan in mind as you write and collect information. It is there to bring new people over to your side with as many facts, figures, and forecasts as you can gather to prove that yes, you are going to be a great big success story.

- **Focus on the six big questions.** To complete your purpose and win over converts, your idea will have to speak for itself and answer six major questions in the business plan: What are you? Why are you? How do you plan to produce results? Whom do you need? When will you deliver on these promises? What will you cost?

- **Don't worry about the format.** Many people worry that they don't know how to put together a business plan. This is the easiest part. Templates of the standard format are available online and in various books.

- **Prepare for changes.** The best business plans show that they can operate and adapt to a variety of circumstances, and are not simply reliant on one fortuitous situation. Make sure you update your business plan as new information comes to mind.

The idea that you can't write a business plan or that it's somehow beyond your capacity is an illusion, just like the Wizard turned out to be. As usual, behind all the pomp and ceremony, all the smoke and mirrors, there is just a regular little man cranking out all of this noise through a machine. Of course, Dorothy and Company had to confront their fears to find out—and you will too. Look at this road-map chapter as your very own yellow brick road, then just follow the advice to go from a blank page to a thick and thorough business plan.

6

ON THE MONEY TRAIL

I ALWAYS LIKED *Seinfeld*. But it wasn't until Jerry Seinfeld decided to end the show that I became curious about Seinfeld the man. Knowing for myself how hard it is to walk away from something at the right time, I wanted to understand where Jerry's inner strength came from. So in May 1998, just as the show was about to go off the air, I bought the *Vanity Fair* that featured him on the cover.

In that article, Jerry said exactly what I'd always felt but had never been able to express about success and making money. In talking about some final negotiations with NBC, he explained: "Some people thought I was stalling, that money was a factor. But in fact I have never considered money. That's the most financially sound approach you can take in my business. When you don't consider money, then you make the right choice. And the right choice always leads to money."

My Story

If I've said it once, I've said it a thousand times . . . I am obsessed with lipstick! I love being able to impart color to my lips, I love seeing color on other people's, I love buying it, and I love owning it. I love the language of lipstick, the camaraderie of lipstick, and the iconography of lipstick. It is and will always be my true cosmetics love. So when I was faced with the decision to go into other cosmetics products under my brand, I felt uneasy.

In the end, the decision was taken out of my hands by a new partner who was determined to make money quickly. Cutting costs and/or growing revenue are the two ways for an existing business to make money. After trimming back the former, he turned his attention to the latter: We needed to boost sales.

It seemed like a no-brainer. If we were doing x amount of sales in the lip category, our business would grow substantially if we offered products in all the cosmetics categories. I can remember putting up some argument, but with my confidence shaken by the events of the last year, which was the year my previous business partners and I ended up in a drawn-out dispute, I didn't have the energy to put up much of a fight. Deep down, I didn't feel right about releasing all these new products. We were doing it for all the wrong reasons. Or rather, we were doing it for only one reason . . . money.

I had no driving force or creative vision for products like liquid foundation, eye shadow, and mascara. These weren't products that enchanted me. There was nothing in particular I wanted to communicate through their colors or textures. There was no message and, worse, there was no passion. We ended up launching an entire line of color cosmetics in one fell swoop. While these had been tweaked according to my taste, they were not labored over by me in labs like the lipstick. Furthermore, to satisfy the cost-cutting element of the strategy, we changed the packaging. In the past, our packaging had been specific to each vignette or story; it was now uniform. Overnight we had become more generic and less quirky because being quirky was at odds with this new faster-buck approach.

While this approach was born of valid financial concerns, it never actually delivered valid financial remedies because it was too weighted toward the one goal of making money. Our customers were not excited about these products. And why should they have been? I wasn't excited about these products either. I am still not sure how I could have thought that the right choice for a brand named Poppy was to create products that left me, Poppy, feeling only lukewarm.

Although Jerry Seinfeld was referring to the entertainment industry in his quote, I would extend what he said to any business or money-related decision. The more you focus on the right choices rather than the right dollars, the more money you are likely to make in the long run. On the flip side, doing things just for the money can have a funny way of backfiring.

LESSON 28: **Ideas need money, and vice versa**

Creativity and money don't always go together. Conventional wisdom has it that creative types are not usually good with money and money types not that creative. So what is more important, money or creativity? On the highway of idea actualization, who gets the right-of-way? Money or ideas? My philosophy says both. Creativity will only take you so far and money alone cannot guarantee something moving. They need each other if either of them is going to go the distance.

To make an idea happen and keep it running, you need a well-tuned mixture of money and creativity. There are times when money will be the focus, and other times when it will have to take a backseat to creativity. The dynamic of any idea is always shifting, rendering neither creativity nor money the ultimate driver. They need to coexist with as much balance as possible.

As you'll find, the emphasis you give each and for what reason will probably be an extension of your philosophy, your values, and your views on the role of money.

My Story

Walking toward a meeting room at the headquarters of Selfridges in London to meet with the cosmetics buyer, I felt a sudden rush of pride when I happened to glance into one of the offices along the corridor. There, up on the bulletin board of their graphic design department, along with other photos and bits and pieces that the designers thought inspirational, was my Shine postcard. This was not the first time this had happened. I had found myself in many different places in the world and seen this card up on the office walls of the hip and fashionable.

Shine was a runaway success. It was 1995, and after a few years of being known for lipstick, I decided to introduce a lip gloss. And not just any old lip gloss, either, but an exaggerated, extreme lip gloss with the wettest, shiniest finish. If lipstick is about glamour, then lip gloss is about sexiness, and mine was going to be R-rated in both look and feel.

This being my first foray away from lipstick, I wanted to make a real statement. The name "Shine" gave it to you straight—the queen of matte was now doing shine. Then the image. I have always loved "truck stop" or airbrush art. Synonymous with the seventies, this was the style that was responsible for those kitschy artificial sunsets, flame decals along the sides of cars and motorbikes, and sexy silhouettes of girls with Jessica Rabbit proportions. It was deliberate fantasy with no claim on anything real or human—and no apologies either. A license to exaggerate, this was the perfect style for the promotional images for Shine.

I found a photo in a magazine with a closeup of a girl's face with big sunglasses and glossy lips. Then I found an airbrush artist to do a hammed-up rendering of this image. Make the sunglasses huge and aviator style. The lips impossibly large and glossy red. The hair loose and wild. Then, put a sunset behind her and have it echoed in the sunglasses. But not just the sunset. This girl was not some beach bunny, but a hip urban chick with her sights set high. New York City. That was the skyline reflected in her glasses, along with all the hopes and dreams that skyline has come to represent.

As to where to put the name of the product, the seventies were once again an inspiration. Remember those necklaces that had a person's name scrolled in a word?

Our girl had the word "Shine" hanging on a necklace.

I spared no expense when it came to the production of this image. We printed large-size posters to go up around the in-store Poppy counters and small postcards to sit next to the Shine display units. If you are not familiar with the economics of the printing world, it goes like this. The less quantity you order, the more expensive it is; and the higher the quality, the higher the price, particularly if it is spread across only a small print run. Our quantities were not large enough to thin out the costs, but I didn't care. I loved this image so much that I refused to settle for anything less than the best-quality paper, the highest resolution of the image, the glossiest finish, the boldest colors, and the best possible option in every choice category.

I justified this as an investment in the brand, and while there is some truth to that, there are also other truths, such as cost of goods; in other words, how much a product costs to produce. Every industry has its standards, and the deluxe spending on production and packaging of this image made the cost of goods on my Shine lip gloss go directly past normal standards, past rationality, and past the business world to the type of thinking that is more appropriate in the art world.

The expenditure was not without its rewards: This image did more for the Poppy brand's cult status than

any other piece of imagery we put out throughout our twelve-year run. Still, could the same results have been achieved within the bounds of conventional economics? Maybe. But I had my foot so heavy on the gas with this one that I refused to use any brakes in the creative surge.

Money needs to respect ideas if it is to keep making money, and ideas need to respect money if they are to reach their potential. No doubt, there are bound to be those times when the money side and creative side are at odds. But once you come to understand their interdependence, you are far less likely to veer away from what is best for both.

LESSON 29: Deciding between financing options

As anyone who's ever tried to order a coffee at Starbucks knows, too much choice can be very complicated. If you need money to make your idea happen, then you have some big choices to make. While your first instinct may be to pursue any and every financial opportunity you can get your hands on, take some time to figure out which options make sense for you before you sign on the dotted line.

Figuring out what makes sense can be very subjective. The truth is that whether you're taking it, making it, giving it, borrowing it, or lending it, money comes with baggage. For the most part, this baggage can be divided into two categories: personal baggage and professional baggage. The former often comes with emotional money, or money that comes from friends, family, acquaintances, neighbors, friends of friends, and so forth. Professional baggage, on the other hand, comes with institutional money—from banks, venture capitalists, organizations, governments, and the like.

The type of financing you choose to pursue will depend on the kind of baggage you're more comfortable with. Both personal and professional have their pros and cons. Emotional money may be easier to find because the criteria for this type of money is not usually all that stringent. For example, Uncle Harry probably won't ask you for as detailed a plan as would a bank. Then again, Harry may have more unrealistic expectations than the bank and he may be assuming that your cousin will get involved as well. Meanwhile, Mr. Bank Loan Administrator is less likely to get hurt feelings if you don't show him enough gratitude or don't employ his cousin—but he is also less likely to take a risk because he has to answer to other people about his decisions.

Before you seek out sources of investment, think about the potential baggage and decide what makes the most sense for you. Are you more comfortable with strict standards and low emotion, or less criteria and more emotion?

ADVENTURES IN BUSINESS

Today's world offers even more opportunity for entrepreneurs than back when I started Poppy Industries. Back then, we had our personal networks, banks, and venture capital (funding from an outside institution in return for equity, or ownership in your company). Venture-capital firms are very narrow in regard to their criteria, and unless you can demonstrate a relatively quick return on the investment, venture capital is nearly impossible to come by. Fortunately, today there's also something I call "adventure capital."

"Adventure capital" comes from a source not only willing to take some risks but actually needing to take these risks to stay competitive. With competition in every market more intense than ever, big behemoths like General Motors are not quite as comfortable with their market position as they were in days of old, when they had no incentive to venture outside their own methods. Nowadays, these companies are opening up to new, less traditional ways of doing business.

If you can offer a company a way to dip its toe into new waters without having to take on a large commitment, you have an interesting proposition. Since trying something new internally can be very costly and complicated, taking a risk on outsiders, with the option to bring them into the fold should the risk pay off, is often more cost effective.

Besides the desire to stay competitive and on top of emerging trends, companies are also motivated to be adventurous if they feel the need to prove something to their market or the general public. Depending on its agenda, a company may want to prove that it is innovative, community-minded, civically responsible, ethnically diverse, gender equal, and so on. If your idea can assist in any of these areas, you may find yourself on the receiving end of either a corporate or government grant. When something you're doing can bring your associates goodwill as well as innovation, you stand a higher chance of getting a company, or even governments or a bank, to finance your idea.

Follow these steps to get through to the corporate decision makers who can help get your idea off the ground:

- **USE THE PHONE.** Call up the corporate offices and ask to speak to someone in the new-ventures or development departments. If they don't have something like this, then ask the switchboard which department they would suggest to pitch an idea to. The person on the phone can help you if you are polite, enthusiastic, and *human*—that is, just be yourself and don't try to act tough.

- **TRY, TRY AGAIN.** If your first attempt to get through to someone doesn't work, then try asking for someone in human resources or brand development or whatever else you can think of. Keep trying to work new angles. You never know when or how you'll hit on someone who will finally point you in the right direction.

- **USE YOUR RESEARCH.** You can often find actual names of the people in charge by looking online. Try researching the corporate Web sites, or go to Google and search for key words like "new development at Subway sandwiches headed up by." When you have your name, go ahead and call. Remember, if your idea is a winner, then you are doing them a service by contacting them. Often, it's much easier than you assume to reach these people. Many people have gotten through to me simply by picking up the phone. *Caution:* There is a line between persistence and stalking. While you will need to be persistent to get through to the busy corporate decision makers, if you have tried to get through to someone for more than three weeks and got nothing . . . move on to the next person or corporation.

LESSON 30: **Speak the language**

If you want to make a good impression, make sure that you're speaking the right language. Just because you may all share the same native tongue doesn't mean there aren't many different vernaculars. Professional, personal, and political sources of money will all respond to different types of wording. So unless the bank manager is also your uncle, don't expect him to take you too seriously if you were to talk to him as such.

For best results, tailor your approach to your audience by figuring out their hot buttons. If you're meeting with a professional or political organization that can provide grants or financing, prepare for the meeting by going over their Web site and literature such as any leaflets or brochures you can find. This is your best chance to get a sense of the concepts that are important to them. When it comes to winning over more personal sources of funding, like good old Uncle Harry, think about the person and what motivates them before launching into your spiel.

Once you've figured out what it is about your idea that would make your audience feel good, you've got your hot buttons. Those are what you should focus on in your meeting.

My Story

About three years after I launched my first seven lipsticks, I had many more lip products and shades. Still, to stay competitive and keep expanding the brand I needed even more new products. Our sales had hit a plateau of about $4 million and if we were to keep growing, we would need more people and ad-

ditional infrastructure, both of which take time and
money. And finding money itself takes time.

I spent most of 1996 on a "road show," slang for doing
presentations over and over again for potential investors.
I met with an endless parade of suits all over Australia—
everyone from wealthy individuals to venture-capital
firms to investment banks to private syndicates. One
place would suggest I see another group, which would
suggest I meet yet another person, and so on.

So every day I would put on my lipstick, gather up
my show and tell, and go sing for my supper. As entertaining as it was for all these people to have some
twenty-four-year-old offer a peek into the world of
female vanities, no one really took my proposition seriously. I had a lot to say but no idea how to say it.

Sure, I could take up a good couple of hours explaining the marketing, the vision, the opportunities,
and the brand positioning. But not in the language of
professional investment. Having had so much success
in communicating my brand to its target market, I just
assumed I was the best person to communicate it to
the investment community. Turns out this is a lot like
assuming that the star of the movie is also the right
person to be the producer. They may be, but only if
they understand the language of both being in a movie
and making one.

As it happened, I didn't know that my words were falling on deaf ears in all these places. I mean, why weren't these suits getting excited about the prospect of bringing downtown glamour to a broader market of postfeminist classic-yet-modern consumers whose psychographic was all about lifestyle?

Wrong language.

Now, if I had been able to hire someone to turn all of that stuff into things like EBITDA, ROI, P&L, and the rest of the acronyms that the professional world of investing speaks in, I may have had more success with the business community. Instead, I wound up getting the investment I needed through a very personal channel, a channel that brought with it a great deal of emotional baggage. Looking back, I realize why I was able to find only the emotional style of investments — it was because that was the only language I knew how to use when presenting my business.

Multilingual. That is what you want to be. While we all have our first language, we can all learn how to speak another tongue well enough to communicate an idea. And if we can't, we need a translator — someone who can help us translate our idea into the proper wording. Depending on which language you speak, that could mean anything from bringing in an MBA with a lot of experience in business start-up to speak with various professional investors to recruiting your more creative, marketing-driven cousin to liven up your presentation when you're looking for financing from friends and relatives.

LESSON 31: Business Partner 101

The business partner is one of the most exotic and adventurous creatures in the finance jungle. Independent from major institutions like banks and investment firms, the business partner is often autonomous and not accountable to large reporting structures. They can roam about freely and fearlessly, hence their sought-after status in the investment wilds. They do not congregate in any one particular habitat but are often found within family, professional connections, friends, networking organizations, and support-group environments. They are also very friendly with Lady Luck, so while you may need her intervention to find one, you don't need to rely on her exclusively since there are steps you can take to improve your chances of meeting potential business partners.

Business partnerships are often compared to marriages — and not for nothing. If you can apply some of the same strategies and principles you would use when looking for a mate to your search for a business partner, you'll be on the right track. For instance:

- **Location, location, location.** To be at the right place at the right time, you have to be at the right place often. Just as people who are looking to meet a life partner would go to bars or online-dating sites, those looking for business partners should go where the sort of people they think of as potential partners may gather.

- **Take initiative.** Once you are fraternizing in the appropriate places, overcome your shyness and put the message out there that you are looking for business partners to help get something off the ground. When I first moved to New York, my sensibilities were shocked by (among other things) people's boldness when it came to matters of the heart (as well as other parts of the anatomy). People would just ask you point-blank if you knew of anyone to set them up with, or if you'd like to be set up with someone they knew. Looking for a business partner requires similar preparedness to put it straight and let people know.

- **Protect yourself.** When it comes to protecting yourself and your idea, you have to figure out what you can say to interest people without revealing too much. During the early business phases, when you're just beginning to gauge interest in your idea, consider applying for a patent and asking people to sign confidentiality agreements before you give away too much information. It's like your mother always said: Anyone who isn't willing to let you use protection can't be right for you.

- **Read the signs.** When looking at potential business partners, you can figure out whether you're a good match or a recipe for disaster by looking out for some common signs. Certain things are essential to good business partnerships, others are nice to have but not absolutely necessary, and still others are potentially problematic. See the "Signs of What's to Come" box for a list of which is which.

My Story

I had no idea what to expect at my initial meeting with the person who ultimately became my first business partner. As I mentioned in an earlier chapter, it was through networking and a mutual connection that I was now sitting in front of someone who had expressed an interest in my idea to start a lipstick brand. It had been a couple of days since we made initial contact. Here I was sitting opposite him at his big glass dining table with a chance at getting my idea off the ground.

There were a lot of clues that were good signs. I

took stock of the surroundings and saw that he loved art and collecting and that his taste leaned toward contemporary, somewhat challenging and confronting. Put it this way: There were no landscapes or still lifes of flowerpots; he obviously liked pushing the envelope. There was also nothing generic around. Everything was unique, and in engaging him in conversation about it, I learned that he deliberately tried to support young and emerging artists and creators. This got us onto the purpose of our meeting.

I told him how I came up with my idea during my own search for matte lipsticks. I explained how I figured out that it was something that many women were looking for, based on the comments I had been getting from sales assistants at cosmetics counters. I told him that I had found a factory that could make them and that I had been in touch with them already. I went on further about whom I thought the market would be for this product, and how and why this lipstick would appeal. It was not exactly a formal presentation, but by covering all the major bases—what the idea was, how it could get done, and for whom—it had the makings of one.

During the meeting, my potential partner asked me some good questions, gave careful and considered responses, and then explained his interest. He told me that he had financed some small ventures in the past because he found it rewarding and exciting to give creative people a go. He was just beginning his law career so he was not interested in anything that would require a full-time commitment. At the end, he said he needed some time to think it through and that he would be traveling for a few weeks, but he would let me know his thoughts when he returned. If he was interested in proceeding, we would need another meeting to talk in more detail. He seemed neither enthusiastic nor particularly indifferent as he thanked me for my time and saw me to the door.

While I was disappointed that I would have to wait a while before I heard back, I had seen some very good signs that I could work with this person. In our first meeting he had proven to be open to risk but not without due consideration. He admired the creative process yet identified that he preferred to act as facilitator rather than creator. He had done these types of ventures before so had some experience in business, and given the fact that he had completed a law degree, he obviously had a degree of structural understanding that would be very helpful. He was polite, respectful, and not only asked questions but listened to my answers. This may seem like very basic stuff, but if you are going to take a leap of faith with someone, and they with you, the devil really is in the details of those early interactions.

When he returned from his trip, he called and wanted to meet again. In a couple of days I was back at his glass table.

"You know what? I think you are right," he said. "I searched for matte lipsticks at all the department stores I went to overseas and no one had them. I was told the same things you were."

Now I knew he meant business. Not many twenty-seven-year-old males I knew were willing to go around asking for lipstick!

Finding a business partner is not as straightforward as, say, getting a loan from a bank. Every business partnership has different dynamics at work. The forms, styles, and expectations are much more varied than they are with institutions that have rigid and set procedures. That is why the search for a successful business partnership shares the same reliance on instincts, impressions, and feelings as do our searches for other extremely important personal relationships in our lives.

SIGNS OF WHAT'S TO COME

As beneficial as business partners could be to your idea, they could also be just as destructive if you happen to choose the wrong partner. To ensure that your partnership has all the makings of a happily ever after, watch out for the following signs:

Essential

- **SHARED VISION.** Whether your business partner is a person, a syndicate, a corporation, or an institution, they must share your vision of the future. This doesn't mean that they have to fully understand every aspect of your business, but you must all share an understanding of its goals. Make sure you hear them describe how they envision the idea and its objectives in their own words. That way any discrepancies will rise to the surface and you can iron them out (or not). No matter how much finance and stability a partnership may bring, if it doesn't come with a shared vision of the overall goals, it is greatly handicapped from day one.

- **SHARED RESPECT.** Respect means you admire someone's skills, talents, experience, and abilities—it doesn't necessarily mean that you like them. Since business partnerships have to weather many ups and downs, respect allows for compromise and communication to triumph over the inevitable differences in opinion. If you can't find anything you truly respect about your potential business partner(s), then reconsider the partnership. It is likely to come to a sticky end. The motto, "Lie down with dogs and you get up with fleas" springs to mind.

- **SHARED DISPUTE RESOLUTION AND EXIT STRATEGIES.** As depressing as it is to talk about the end when you're only at the beginning, you need to have a shared sense of how that end could happen. For example, after a certain time frame, will one party have the option to sell to another? What will you do if there is a dispute or a stalemate? There are many well-used and accepted exit and dispute resolution strategies at your disposal. Your best bet is to agree upon which ones you would use before you even begin. In the unfortunate event that your business partnership gets into trouble, frustration may be too high and camaraderie too low for parties to think clearly.

Nice to Have

- **SHARED VALUES.** History has shown some successful partnerships between some rather odd couples. For instance, you can still have a great business partnership with someone who has different religious beliefs, follows a different sports team, or votes for a different political party—just look at Bill Clinton and George Bush senior, who have joined forces on many causes recently. Sharing personal values may be very helpful, but it's no guarantee that the business partnership will be a success. Remember, just because you have great dinner table conversations with your business partner doesn't mean you can make a real go of a professional arrangement. It is more important that you agree on the strategy of the business rather than say, the strategy of the Mets.

Potentially Problematic

• **SHARED SKILLS.** Ideally you want your business partnership to round out your skill set and bring new expertise to the endeavor. Too many shared skills can cause complications and duplications in the roles that individuals play within the partnership. Clear distinction and separation of skills will not only help with the execution of your idea but will minimize the potential of territorial politics. Draining and time-consuming internal wrangling and power struggles take attention away from the real goals of the partnership.

• **DIFFERENT EXPECTATIONS.** Make sure that what each entity in the partnership expects, and in what time frame, is clear from the start. Even if you have a shared vision, there may be differences in how and when one party expects that vision to be realized. Something as simple as timing can make a strong partnership come unglued if the expectations around this aren't agreed upon and satisfactory to all those involved.

In the beginning, a lot of information can be gleaned from the gestures. Before you get up and running with a partnership, have a good look and think about the gestures or signs you are seeing—while there are no guarantees, you should have enough clues to make an educated decision.

LESSON 32: Sometimes, a dollar is more than just a dollar

A good deal doesn't always mean a good value. Capital (finance or money) itself can be value added. For example, $50,000 from one source may be very different than

$50,000 from another. What does the money come with? Does it come with expertise or infrastructure that could be helpful to you above and beyond the money alone? Or does it come from a source that has no real synergies or experience in the field of your idea? Are there any efficiencies that could be shared or absorbed, such as a sales force that you could use to sell something of yours? A dollar doesn't always have to be worth exactly one hundred cents—not when it comes with a whole lot of extras built in.

Now, as to whether that dollar is worth more or less depends on the nature of the extras tacked on. After all, not all extras are beneficial. For instance, will someone's friend be appointed to manage the business? If so, why and what is their experience? For capital to be truly value added it doesn't just mean that other stuff comes with it, it means that the right stuff comes with it. And by right stuff, I mean expertise, knowledge, or support systems that will really help you.

And remember, sometimes the best deals are not necessarily the best for you. It's easy to get caught up in the hunt for the deal and forget all about what you really need. This happens to me every time I shop at Century 21, the famous designer discount store in New York. I get so carried away with the bargains that I often buy outfits that wind up at the nearest Goodwill store after only a brief stint in my closet. So keep in mind, even if you get a good deal, if the value is all in the deal alone, you may be better off looking for capital that brings with it more than just a bargain.

My Story

There was a point when I thought any deal would be better than no deal at all. I was wrong. The business had some major problems due to speedy growth, sales plateaus, competition, and poor internal management decisions (not the least of which were my own).

This was all happening while I was on my road show, searching high and low for investment, and struggling because I hadn't yet figured out how to find it. I thought that all the business needed was money to bridge the gap between our opportunities and our piggy bank. I finally found it through a connection.

Other than a genuine desire to make things work, there really wasn't any synergy. Unfortunately, best intentions do not a best business make, and the partnership turned sour and became a problem well beyond finance.

It got so bad that we all ended up in the hands of the bank, which, in turn, brought in their own people to manage a crisis that had now escalated into a stand-off between parties over the way to move forward. Through this process I was exposed to some very smart people at the firm of KPMG. People who had enormous experience and knowledge in steering businesses through hardship and who knew of workable options available to businesses that had become destabilized.

After dealing with these very capable, strategic thinkers, I realized what I wish I'd known at the start of my partner search—that what I really needed was expertise rather than finance.

In the world of funding, all that glitters is not gold. When you're comparison shopping, don't forget that ten dollars from an experienced and knowledgeable source may have more value than a hundred from a source that doesn't bring valuable expertise.

LESSON 33: Ownership isn't everything

Ownership. The single most controversial and provocative word in the business vernacular. Who has it? How much? Why and for how long?

The very idea of ownership is deeply entwined in the

human psyche. Our instincts are to protect our ownership at all costs because the more ownership you have,
the more control you have as well. However, ownership
itself is not always the best way to achieve success. You
can own and control a whole business that isn't a success, or you could own a small percentage of a business
that is. Now think about it: Would you still prefer to have
the whole pie even if it is a mess, or would you prefer a
smaller slice of something that is much tastier?

Different sources of funding will bring with them different ownership structures. If the funding is truly value
added, as we discussed above, it may be worth considering sacrificing some ownership to have expertise involved
that can really help give your idea its best shot. The best
type of funding will be clear about where your skills lie
and your value to the big picture, and should show they
understand this by giving you substantial ownership in
the areas that you are best at. This may not translate to
ownership overall, but it may translate to a much health-
ier proposition.

My Story

"Hello, Poppy Industries."

That was the standard greeting you received when
you phoned my business. Often, when there were

many lines ringing and the receptionist was busy, I would pick up a line and say it myself.

It felt good to answer a phone with the words "Poppy Industries." That's right. My business. My creation. I had dreamed this up and now it was a full-blown operation with real people, real phone lines ringing, and real callers on the other end. Sometimes, I felt so proud to be the Poppy of Poppy Industries. Other times, I felt terrified. There were moments when I would look at the staff leaving and wish that I too could go home without feeling like this whole thing was my responsibility. Anyone who owns and operates an organization feels like this at times regardless of the size and complexities. It is easy to develop a case of "grass is greener" blues.

I had some wonderful staff and great support, but the times that the words "Poppy Industries" felt most daunting were the times when what I really needed was help—help in the form of other people who owned this thing along with me. I needed strong, knowledgeable experience from someone who, like me, was invested in an ownership capacity and also needed successful outcomes for the company. But at twenty-four, I was on my own. I owned both a multi-million-dollar company and the multimillion-dollar headache to match.

When time comes to divide up the ownership, try not to get obsessed with how you can set yourself up for the most, and focus instead on how you are going to set yourself up for the best. This may sound like some cheesy take-home exercise from a team-building weekend filled with platitudes and rope courses, but the fact is that taking on less may allow you to do better overall. The more everyone is focused on their individual direction, the more successful the outcome will be.

Conclusion

You may have noticed that for a chapter about money I have talked a lot about happiness. It is true that money can't buy happiness, but happiness can very often make money. The happier you are with whatever financial arrangements you get involved in and whom they bring with them, the more effective you will be. But be prepared: Happiness isn't the same as comfort. Contrary to what you may think, money is not the antidote to the jitters. People are. Solid relationships are. The better you feel about your relationship with money and the people, places, and things that come with it, the better your judgment is likely to be.

When you enjoy what you do, your happiness is contagious. Don't let financial burdens keep you from taking pleasure in what you're doing. Remember to:

- **Balance between money and ideas.** For a business to survive, money and ideas need to coexist peacefully. Whether you're idea-driven or money-motivated, make sure you're not favoring either side at the expense of the other when making business decisions.
- **Weigh your financing options.** If you can't afford to bankroll your own idea, you're going to have to look for investors. Personal loans and professional loans come with different types of requirements, so figure out which type of investment would make you more comfortable before signing on the dotted line.
- **Use appropriate language.** Just because you have an idea, a passion, and a way with words doesn't mean that you know how to present your idea. Think of your audience's needs and concerns. Then adjust your language accordingly. If you can't, bring in someone who can.
- **Evaluate potential business partners carefully.** When I say carefully, I mean as carefully as you would a potential spouse, because *that* is how vital a role your business partner will play in your professional life.

Use all your senses to find someone who is compatible.

- **Take the extras into consideration.** Besides money, every potential deal brings its own assets and liabilities, benefits and drawbacks. These are the extras. Instead of focusing too much on the dollar amounts, take these extras into consideration when deciding whether or not to join forces with potential investors.

- **Avoid getting too caught up in the idea of ownership.** Some entrepreneurs get so caught up in the idea of ownership that they forget that owning a minority stake in something good is better than owning the majority of nothing much. When you're going over deals and talking contracts, remember that this isn't about getting the most, but the best—and sometimes that means taking a smaller share of the pie.

During his long tenure as chairman of the U.S. Federal Reserve, Alan Greenspan became something of a cult figure. Not only did he preside over some amazing periods in the U.S. economy, from the stock market crash of 1987 to the Internet bubble and the Enron and World-Com collapses, but he had an enigmatic persona and a lofty use of language that spawned some great quotes.

Two of his most famous were "irrational exuberance" (to describe the dot-com frenzy) and "infectious greed" (to describe the corporate scandals). On numerous occasions, it's occurred to me that if you take the best elements of these two quotes and put them together, you get a winning formula for making and finding money: infectious exuberance!

7

MARKETING:

ANYONE CAN DO IT

NOT LONG AGO, I was standing in line at a drugstore when an ad came on and interrupted the sounds of the Muzak being piped through the sound system.

"Have you tried the Kabbalah Energy Drink?" the upbeat voice asked.

I didn't hear the rest because the guy behind me and I looked at each other, laughed, and shook our heads with incredulous amazement. As the most lofty and mysterious of Judaism's teachings, the kabbalah is not something one would immediately associate with "a delicious citrus fusion which contains essential vitamins and amino acids that pick you up and keep you going."

Of course, that only goes to show that marketing is

everywhere—even in areas where I would suggest it has no business being. Still, I firmly believe that you don't have to abuse the system to use the system. In a world where messages are coming at us 24/7, from every available surface and through every imaginable medium, you have to decide whether to be a passive receiver or an active player. Regardless of what it is you want to do, from designing your own lipstick brand to moving up the corporate ladder, the more conscious you are about the messages you put out, the better you will set yourself up for success.

My Story

I'll never forget how excited I was the first time I headed out to see the lipstick factory after having found it in the phone book. Aladdin's cave here I come, I thought.

But when I got there, it wasn't at all what I expected. Where was the secret entrance? Who hid the massive control panel? And what happened to all the velvet? I realize I was only seventeen, but wouldn't you expect some velvet at a lipstick factory?

I also had to get over the fact that the people at the helm were not a bunch of suave James Bond types and devastating femme fatales, but the kind of regular people you'd find trolling the aisles of a supermarket.

Turns out all this was just work, another chore, not a crusade on behalf of the powers of lipstick seduction.

The final shock arrived when I saw how lipstick was made. Apparently, lipstick is just a mixture of powders, pigments, oils, and waxes. That's it! I am not saying it is easy to get it right, but the stuff itself is just so basic. Somehow I was expecting more. Some magic. Some ancient secret of a concoction. But no . . . All the fuss and money that lipstick generates can all be traced back to highly unglamorous factories.

I could hardly believe it. All those times my heart had beat a little faster when buying a lipstick. Those times in front of the mirror when I put it on and felt instantly transformed into a more sophisticated woman. The fixation on finding that perfect color that would make Tom or Bill or Josh or whomever I had a crush on at the time suddenly take notice of me. The proud feeling that I had arrived as a female when I was finally allowed to wear it. All those hopes and dreams that this product carried not just for me but for billions of women all over the world. And here I was confronted with the reality that all of the above had absolutely nothing to do with the product itself and everything to do with the expectations and suggestions surrounding it.

The word "marketing" has such a technical ring to it that many people are scared off by its implications. PhDs in white lab coats. Focus groups. Statistics. These are just a few of the images that come to mind. But contrary to popular belief, marketing's greatest successes don't come out of market research firms but out of empathy. The best marketing is all about appealing to people's needs and wants, be they vain and irrational or sensible and practical. Now, how do you figure out what those needs and wants are? You look at your own needs and wants. It's that simple. You don't need focus groups.

WE'RE ALL MARKETING GURUS

While perfecting your marketing skills may take some practice, you can start right now with a product that we all own, a product that is always changing and has unlimited potential for growth. It is the one product that can't be ripped off, knocked off, or pulled off by anyone else. As you may have guessed, that product is none other than you. Whatever you do, there's no brand of person quite like you.

Whether you're marketing yourself at work or in your social life, the underlying theme is the same: There's the product, in this case you, and there's the customer you're trying to sell yourself to, whether that be your boss, a love interest, or a potential friend. Chances are, you've already marketed yourself many times over by using some of the following techniques:

- Writing a resume
- Going on job interviews
- Getting dressed
- Telling jokes
- Playing "hard to get"
- Putting in extra time at work without being asked

In all of these instances and many others, you're trying to send the message that you can be an asset and provide a benefit of some kind. As you'll no doubt discover, the more conscious you are of the message you are trying to send, the more effective you will be.

LESSON 34: **Keep it real**

When setting out to become a marketing expert, make sure to stay a human being. Never forget that your targets are people first and an audience second. Whether you want to use marketing to get the attention of consumers or the attention of your boss, whether your audience consists of one person or one hundred thousand, you're always dealing with human beings just like you.

There are a great deal of helpful marketing theories, buzzwords, and formulas. While these are all very interesting to consider, they are no substitute for your own thoughts and feelings. A marketing expert is really just another way of describing someone who is very trusting of their intuition. Someone who is so keenly aware of their own reactions to people, places, and situations, that they become very good at predicting the reactions of others.

When you focus on understanding yourself and pay attention to your own thoughts and feelings, you naturally become more understanding and compassionate of others. As that happens, it becomes easier and easier to design messages that will produce the reactions you seek.

My Story

About four years into my business, the reputation and legend of the lipsticks had spread to places as diverse

as South Africa, Russia, and India. I had all sorts of approaches from people who wanted to represent the brand in these countries, but the most aggressive approach came from a very placid corner of the world — Canada. One day my brother received a phone call from a guy in Montreal who told him he had registered the Poppy brand name in Canada. If we ever wanted to do business there, he said we had to partner with him. No, it wasn't Tony Soprano.

As it turned out, this rather kneecap-breaking style of introducing himself was really just this guy's way of showing how much he believed. My brother explained that we didn't have the resources to open new markets and that we were actually in the process of looking for an injection of funding before we could consider new opportunities.

"In that case," he said, "come to Canada and meet with me and my dad. We have so many connections. Perhaps we can help you." After a little research into him and his family, that was exactly what we did. On the next business trip to meet with Barneys, I included a stop in Canada.

He picked us up from the airport and whisked us off to his family's immense weekend estate. The plan was to spend the weekend brainstorming on the strategy of the brand and then to brainstorm about finding investment. Around lunchtime the earth began to tremble as an ominous whirring noise became louder and louder. But it was just his dad. Arriving in his helicopter.

His father was like someone sent from central casting to play the role of rugged, debonair megamillionaire. He looked, dressed, and sounded the part. Not one to mince words, he gave me his opinion whether I wanted it or not. At one point, he asked if we wanted to go for a dip. Then, instead of hopping in the car, we piled into the chopper and flew to a lovely swimming spot. Once we were airborne he leaned over to me (and if he didn't have a cigar between his teeth, he should have) and said, "How much do you think this thing costs to fly for five minutes?" I can't remember the number, but it was astounding. He laughed when he saw the shock on my face, and that was him, a big kid with big toys.

If it sounds like I fell in love with him a bit that weekend, that's because I sort of did. It wasn't just his intriguing personality or the thrilling situation, but his sound advice and fantastic stories. The one I will always remember is about a successful entrepreneur who had made tons of money from those airplane catalogs you find in the seat pockets. I always end up flipping through them out of boredom and that's exactly what this guy had caught on to: Planes have captive audiences with nothing better to do than order a dog feeder that also doubles as a plant holder. With his catalog business thriving, he decided to edge out any competition by taking his service one step further: Instead of having the products delivered through the mail, his customers could receive them at the airport. *Ta da!* Immediate gratification.

Sounds like a good idea, right? So he invested in warehousing close to airports and set up a system that could register the order while the customer was on the plane and then deliver the product upon landing. And what do you think happened?

He lost a huge amount of money, that's what. The idea seemed great in theory, but in reality, the first thing people want to do when they hit an airport is get the heck out of there. They do not want more packages to lug, more counters to visit, or more time to spend waiting if for some reason they landed before the goods arrived. Now, if this guy had thought about his own experiences as a traveler, he may have realized he didn't want to spend any more time in airports than he absolutely had to. Neither would his customers, as they were not alien beings but people just like him, flying around the same universe as he was.

Don't lose yourself in grand plots, schemes, and theories. Focus on reality. You could drive yourself nuts trying to incorporate all the different marketing philosophies, or you can market the sane way—through empathy. Empathy isn't found in diagrams, statistics, graphs, or charts, but within yourself. Look at how you respond and react to experiences, then trust in the fact that you are not alone. If you're feeling and thinking something, there is an army of others who must be feeling and thinking the same thing.

LESSONS 35–38: The Four Elements of Successful Marketing

While there may not be any sure things in the world of marketing, there are certain indicators of success. Most successful marketing campaigns can be described as:

- Simple
- True
- Consistent
- Having a point of view

These four points may be easier to remember if you incorporate them into the popular wedding-related rhyme, "something old, something new, something borrowed, something blue"—in other words: **"Something simple, something true, something consistent, and something with a point of view."**

While there are no guarantees, you can think of these four elements as a great start and try to keep them in mind while you work on getting your message across.

LESSON 35: **Something simple**

In a world where speed and clarity are in demand, complicated messages are nowhere near as successful as the simple ones. Among the many messages bombarding us every day, two are emerging as the most resonant—value and validation. To market successfully, you have to fall into one of these two camps. Value means good return for the money; this type of marketing appeals to our practical, budget-conscious, and fiscally responsible side. Validation is more emotion-driven in that in some way the product comes with certain benefits that make you want to pay a premium.

Let's take Starbucks and Dunkin' Donuts coffee as examples. In the *Economist,* Internet entrepreneur Tom McInerney was quoted as saying, "Starbucks has comfy chairs but they don't charge people for sitting in them. Instead they provide this comfortable environment at considerable expense so that people will buy overpriced coffee." Conversely, Dunkin' Donuts has been successful with its lower-priced coffee by using the exact opposite message — no frills, just good coffee.

Both the value and validation messages have their own sets of pros and cons. But you'll have to choose a side. With value messages, you get to offer consumers a good deal, but you'll have to move a lot of product to compensate for the lower price. If you're working the validation message angle, you will have to invest a lot more into convincing people that you've got what they need. While this message can be a lot more expensive to communicate, you can charge double, triple, or ten times as much for the validating feelings that come with your product or service.

Whatever your strategy, the key is to choose one message and make it very simple for the customer to understand where you're coming from. There should be no room for confusion.

My Story

Australia is known for its beaches, its lifestyle, and its athletic, outdoorsy denizens. What is less known about Australia is something called the "cultural cringe." This refers to the unfortunate fact that in certain industries — fashion and cosmetics particularly — Australian consumers are much more likely to believe in imported products over local ones.

While this trend has been reversed in the past decade, when I first started my lipstick brand back in 1992, it was in full swing. At the time, the only Australian-made cosmetics on the market were very cheap and did not dare compete with the U.S. or French brands. Relegated to the bargain sections in the back of the stores, Australian companies were considered vastly inferior to foreign brands like Estée Lauder and Lancôme.

Given that this was the mentality the manufacturers of my lipsticks were used to, you can imagine their disbelief when I told them I was going to charge a price that put us smack down alongside the VIPs.

"Do you really think people will pay that much for an Australian lipstick?" they asked.

"They will if they know it is special," I answered.

I was sure that if I fulfilled my end of the deal and made my customers feel the product was special, then they would fulfill theirs and pay a little extra. I was clear that my main priority was communicating the "specialness" first, and everything else would follow. With that in mind I was able to keep things fairly simple when it came to my marketing decisions. Did this contribute to the "special factor" or take away from it? Anything that did the latter had to go. The clearer this was to me, the clearer it would be to the customer.

I'll never forget the day I realized I had succeeded in making my brand as highly regarded as the imports. An associate and I were driving along the highway toward my lipstick manufacturers. In the lane next to us was a school bus filled with teenage schoolgirls in navy and yellow uniforms. One of them saw me in the car and started shouting "Hey, it's Poppy!" But all that showed was that I had succeeded in self-promotion, not in communicating the brand's message. It was what they did next that proved to me that my brand had become not just something to buy, but something to believe in and feel good about. Out of nowhere, about ten or fifteen of the girls started waving Poppy lipstick brochures out the window like flags. Now, that was some moment for me!

Whether you're aiming to position yourself in the labor market or in the consumer market, you'll be at an advantage if you can clearly articulate what it is that you do very, very well rather than trying to show that you can do and be everything. Remember, keeping a message simple is not about dulling and diffusing it by trying to be all things to everyone, but sharpening it to the kind of point that can hit a bull's-eye rather than just anywhere on the bull.

LESSON 36: **Something true**

Truth is at the core of any successful long-term marketing program. It may not be a truth you admire, but it is a truth nonetheless. Customers, consumers, and audiences are not idiots. They can spot the difference between fake and authentic. Good marketing is about delivering something real and building on that connection.

The real, authentic, and genuine is much more likely to lead to a successful endeavor not because it's ethical but because it is logical. It stands to reason that the closer your message is to a truth, the stronger and more hard-hitting it will be. Now, contrary to conventional wisdom, truth doesn't have to be noble or right or just—it just has to be true in some way, shape, or form. So don't worry about how noble your message is . . . just worry about how true it is. In other words, the way forward will be much clearer if you let truth determine the message and not the other way around.

ONE TRUE THING

In *A Moveable Feast,* Ernest Hemingway writes about how he breaks bouts of writer's block. He tells himself to just "write one true sentence. Write the truest sentence you know." I can't tell you how much this insight has helped me in times of blockage, fear, and crisis of confidence. If I can't figure out what to do next, I concentrate on writing down the most true thing about what it is I am trying to do and it helps. As Hemingway said, "So finally I would write one true sentence and then go on from there. It was easy then."

Now it's your turn. What is the truest thing you can say about what you're trying to do? Take a moment and write it down.

My Story

The cosmetics floor of Australian department stores in the early nineties reminded me of a school playground. As soon as the bell rang, all the kids would spill out onto the playground and branch off into groups according to their social milieu. Every size, shape, and style of kid was represented, and each gravitated toward their own kind. Had the cosmetics department been the school yard, though, I wouldn't have known whom to hang out with.

I really didn't fit in with any of the gangs. Dior, Estée Lauder, and Lancôme were too posh for me. Clarins and Clinique were too neat with their surgical outfits. Maybelline and Cutex were too chirpy. And then there were the really trashy gangs who shall remain nameless. Not one of these brands felt like a species I could relate to. None of them had any sense of humor, especially not when it came to themselves. These brands were all institutionalized and very corporate.

When it came time to marketing my own brand I got scared at times (just like I did at school) that I wouldn't be able to be both weird and popular, and that I would have to make my brand fit in with these corporate types. But that went directly against the truest sentence I could think of to say about my brand, which was:

It's not corporate.

I had a choice. I could try to make my brand look all stitched up and perfect like the others, or I could accept that mine was going to be a bit messy and strange looking. Then it dawned on me. Of course! I should do more than just accept that I wasn't corporate. If that was the truth then I should really market this aspect, and hope that by telling my truth more people would respond rather than less.

And they did. It may not have been perfect, but it was genuine and it drew people from all over — often,

people who I never would have even expected to respond to my quirky little brand. I'll never forget the
conspiratorial grin on the face of one very elderly lady
(she must have been over eighty) who came up to one
of my counters. She leaned into me, reeking of moth-
balls and powder, and with one hand on my forearm
and the other steadying herself on the bench, she said,
"I'll have two tubes of Lust lipstick."

The saying "the truth will set you free" holds doubly true
for marketing. The more real your message, the more appealing it will be. Just as importantly, if you figure out
your most authentic aspect, you will be able to look ahead
and make decisions based on that truth. If you don't, you'll
spend your whole time trying to fit in and letting others
dictate your direction, like a preteen on a playground.
And that, simply put, is not authentic. It's not true. And
it's not good marketing.

LESSON 37: **Something consistent**

Being consistent is one of the most underestimated and
overlooked factors of a successful marketing strategy. Everyone loves to point to the mavericks, the pioneers, the
enfants terribles as the heroes of marketing, but it is consistency that can really save the day. More than any other

quality, consistency is what allows people to trust in you, your products, or your services. So remember, "repetition, repetition, repetition" is to marketing what "location, location, location" is to real estate — an enormous asset.

Consistency sounds boring, but it doesn't have to be. After all, it's not the delivery that needs to stay consistent but only the underlying message. You can come up with exciting and varied marketing campaigns that all share the same message. Take Gucci, for example. During the nineties, the design house revamped its faded image to much success — all without ever changing its core message of being upscale, aspirational, and empowering.

Keep in mind that it takes a long time to lodge a message, but only a short time to dislodge it. Think of your customer's, client's, or boss's mind as a savings account: You need to make consistent deposits of a message over a period of time before you build up enough of a bank balance to have an impact. But it takes only a few radical spending sprees to get you back to zero.

My Story

Here's a thought . . . why don't you play teacher and grade me on this one. The score you give me will depend on whether you view this part of my story as consistent with the rebel message of my brand or completely inconsistent with the fun message of my brand. I myself remain fairly undecided to this day.

Everything was going so well. We were turning over millions in lipsticks and the Poppy brand was entrenched in Australian folklore. As I mentioned previously, I was awarded Young Australian of the Year in 1995, and without even thinking about the consequences, I started weighing in on weighty matters well outside the fashion and cosmetics arena. I had always been a fairly pushy little thing, unwilling to take no for an answer, and now I had a national stage from which to pester people about things that were important to me.

So as soon as I heard that there was a movement starting for Australia to become a republic, I got on board. Quick lesson for you on the Australian constitution: As it stands, the ruling monarch of England (at present Queen Elizabeth) is also Australia's queen and is therefore head of state. She holds the highest possible Australian office without even being Australian herself. Now I have nothing against the woman personally—in fact, I find a lot to admire about her— but I am against the idea that Australia still needs to hold on to England's coattails. Despite our strong historical connection to the UK, we are now our own independent country and I, among others, wanted to recognize this by changing the constitution.

Leaping into this hotbed of a debate headfirst, I gave speeches on the subject in school assemblies, churches, and town halls all over the country. I became publicly aligned with other high-profile members of this movement. In the end, I'd become almost as well known for my support of the movement as I was for lipstick. And therein lay the trouble.

First, any debate has both supporters and detractors. I must have alienated many customers who did not share my support for the cause. Second, lipsticks are a message related to fun, fashion, color, and femininity. Political causes carry an entirely different message. They may be okay for someone like Anita Roddick, who started the Body Shop based on a core environmental and political message, but my brand had an entirely different mood—a mood inconsistent with the raging emotions surrounding the country's constitutional future.

So teacher, what do you think? Give me a C for consistency (or even an F)? Or a B for bravery? It's a judgment call. While there is admiration for the cause, my actions did damage me and the brand in the consistency area. Was I in business or in politics? Was it all about fun fashion or serious issues? Good intentions or not, any time you squeeze a new message into the party, the original ones get pushed into a corner.

You don't have to be the best at marketing to be good at it. In fact, you can get more mileage from being amazingly consistent rather than consistently amazing. In *Dangerous Liaisons,* one of my favorite movies, the character played by John Malkovich replies to Glenn Close's character's haughty assertion that she is the best at something by saying, "Yes, but it is always the best swimmers who drown." Keep this quote in mind as you market yourself. While overconfidence can push you to overexperiment, consistency will keep you anchored by reminding you never to take the bond between your audience and your message for granted. No message is so strong that it can survive without consistent reinforcement.

LESSON 38: **Something with a point of view**

I have a fabulous pair of slippers that I bought on a trip to India. The toe curls backward not just once but three times and there is so much elaborate work on them that they are more for decoration than anything else. Every time I look at them I think of the guy I bought them from. When I asked him what size they were, he replied: "What size are you?" Wise to his game, I wouldn't tell him. I just kept asking what size the shoes were and we were both smiling as neither of us would give in. Instead of a Mexican standoff this was an Indian standoff, shoe-shopping style. I knew that whatever size I said, he would tell me the shoes were the same.

Although I wound up buying the shoes, being whatever your customer wants you to be is not a strategy I would ever recommend. For marketing to be successful it needs a point of view, or something that is identifiably yours. Now, this doesn't necessarily mean you have to be different to be successful, but it does mean that you have to be well defined.

Much like the area you live in, your point of view tells your customer what you believe and where you belong. When it comes to marketing, there are very few unpopulated areas. Pretty much everything has been covered, and that's okay. As long as you have something to say, it doesn't have to be something completely new and unheard of.

My Story

I have amnesia when it comes to jokes and acronyms. I am sure I have been told many jokes over my lifetime, but whenever I am asked to tell a joke I can only recall one or two. Where did all the others go? The same goes for acronyms, those letters that are used to stand for something, like KFC for Kentucky Fried Chicken. In business, there are thousands of these. And still, no matter how many times I am told what the letters represent, I can't seem to retain the information. However, there is one that I always remember: AUS. It stands for average unit sale, which is the average amount of money people spend on something.

Cosmetics brands are obsessed with the AUS and getting it to go up. Of course they want customers to buy more from them each time; why wouldn't they? I am sure that is why the people behind their counters wear so many of their products. The more layers of makeup you insist people wear, the more they spend.

Just try asking a cosmetics counter person what eyeliner she (or he) is wearing and you'll no doubt hear not only about the liner but the different eye shadows, powders, and mascaras that set it off to its best advantage. Before you know it they have a big AUS and you have a whole lot of junk that you never wear.

When it comes to makeup, my point of view has been and always will be that you play up either your lips or your eyes—never both.

This method has become trendy recently and has even been given its own name—"zoning," or focusing on one area of the face. Just like everything trendy, I am sure next season the magazines will move on to something else. For all I know, "piling" could become the new thing and we'll all be urged to pile on as much as possible.

As a cosmetics marketer, I could drive myself mad trying to respond to every trend, so my point of view has been not to try. I have stuck to this same method with my customers for years, and although I have made adjustments to suit different moods, I have never wandered from my area.

What I lost in AUS I made up for in CRED (as in credibility). One day, I was at one of my counters, helping a lady who wanted advice on makeup to go with the dress she was wearing to her daughter's wedding. We found the perfect shade of lipstick and she was thrilled.

"Which of your lip liners should I wear to go with this?" she asked.

"Do you want to change the shape of your lips or have trouble keeping lipstick on?" I asked, after looking at her lips.

"Neither, but I've always been told that you had to wear a lip liner with lipstick."

I explained that in her case then it wasn't necessary. She looked somewhat surprised, thanked me, and went on her way.

About half an hour later, she was back. She bought three more lipsticks, saying she was so impressed with my fresh approach that she felt the urge to come back and buy more.

If you have ever lived with a cat, you may have seen them moving round and round in a circle before deciding exactly where to sit. Once they've picked a spot, though, you can't budge them. That's what a marketing point of view should be like. Circle around the vicinity where you are looking to market, then decide on what it is you are saying, and sit on it.

Conclusion

One of the most intimidating aspects of marketing is the idea that you have to come up with "the next big thing." Whenever I think of it like that I seize up entirely. But I always relax when I realize that the next big thing is actually the same old things that have always worked. The more you can market something in a simple, believable, consistent, and clear manner, the better a marketer you will be, whether it is a product you are marketing or your own skills.

In the end, effective marketing is really just about putting your best foot forward by making sure that the message you are sending out is in line with what you stand for. You can do that by:

- **Staying human.** Don't get so caught up in the volumes of marketing theory that you forget what marketing is all about—connecting with people. Get in touch with your own emotions and you'll have more success when trying to reach out to others.

- **Remembering the four keys to marketing.** "Something simple, something true, something consistent, and something with a point of view." Keep these four cornerstones of good marketing at the forefront of your mind when you're planning and strategizing.

To be a great marketer, you need only be honest with yourself. People are more alike than they are different, so once you understand what drives your behavior—from the silliest to the wisest of motives—you can give people what they want. And that, in a nutshell, is the essence of good marketing. No lab coat required!

8

PUTTING YOURSELF

ON THE LINE

I ONCE GOT beaten up by a kangaroo. It was a mascot for a tourist restaurant in Central Australia and I was three years old at the time. I followed it around desperate to hug it, to show it the full extent of my amorous feelings. It got so sick of me it turned around and socked me one. There are certain situations that require certain moderation with feelings. Developing an idea involves good management with them. Feelings are simply not a part of professional vernacular. The elephant in the room, emotions are a cumbersome liability in the work world, rumored to exist but best forgotten. To help us forget, lots of neat euphemisms have been concocted to replace the need to mention you know what. Words like "productivity," "incentivizing," "key performance indicators," "goals," and "targets" are the sanitized versions of "hopes," "dreams," "happiness," "fulfillment," and "desire."

Despite these efforts on behalf of corporations the world over, there's still no getting around the fact that to get any idea off the ground—whether it's a business or a move up the corporate ladder—you'll have to invest feelings as well as effort. In fact, oftentimes, you may find that managing your feelings seems like a primary job responsibility.

My Story

It was 1998. My day would start around 5 AM—not because I wanted it to, but because I was having trouble sleeping. It was still dark when I would walk the short distance to the corner store to buy the newspapers. The guy behind the counter looked sheepish and apologetic as soon as he saw me. With his eyes averted he would hand me my change with a What can you do? sigh.

The reason for his behavior was this: Every single day for approximately three months running, the papers carried a new story about the dispute between me and my business partners—often on the front page. It is hard to describe the feelings of helplessness and frustration that come with reading horrible articles about yourself that you know in a few hours' time the entire country would be waking up to see.

The hardest part about it was not that these articles were written, but the slanted reporting. Given that the company was in trouble at this stage, the attacks on my business skills and decisions were understandable, but I could not reconcile myself to the attacks on my character. They were vicious. More vicious than I could ever have imagined.

I remember one day, I was going through an especially tough time and wanted to get out of my office for some fresh air. This was one of those rare days when there were no reporters camped in the street, so I was able to wander down to the 7-Eleven without being bothered. Outside the store was one of those newspaper sheets that have the lead story and headline of the day. There it was in huge, bold letters: *Poppy to Go to Court.* The paper had run an article based on nothing but rumor, saying that I was to stand trial on some white-collar charge.

It was completely untrue.

I felt sick to my stomach. Then even more so when I saw the discomfort on the faces of everyone in the store as I walked past this poster. "It should have said 'Poppy to go to 7-Eleven,'" I said. This was my feeble attempt at humor to ease the tension of the moment.

During those days I took heart in whatever it was that could get me from one hour to the next. The support of people who really knew me was crucial, but so was that of those who didn't know me but reached out to wish me the best all the same. One of these letters is as etched into my mind as if it came yesterday. It was from a very well-known feminist scholar who had experienced her own fair share of infamy.

"I wanted to write to you to let you know how disturbed I am with the media surrounding your business woes," she wrote. "I have never seen anything like this level of attack on someone who has not actually been guilty of anything other than a problematic business partnership. I am shocked and horrified at the treatment you're being given by our media."

In my reply, I wrote:

Thank you so much for your letter. It meant a great deal to me, more than you can ever know. Please take heart in the fact that the only things the media can take from me are the things that I have come now to understand mean very little. They can take my fame, my status, my ability to get the best table at a restaurant, and my place on the A list. They can assist in the demise of any fortune I may have and they can assist in the demise of my outside credibility.

As much as all of the above hurts (and it does!), I know my own motives, my own actions, and my own mistakes. Although I have been stupid at times in my business, I have never been deceitful. And as long as I know that when my head hits the pillow at night, there is nothing lasting that the media can ever really do to me. I thank you so much for your kindness and support.

When I reread what I'd written, I was surprised to realize that I'd meant every word. It had been easy to say that money, prestige, and fame don't matter when I was riding high, but no one can know that for sure until they stand to lose it. So I was very relieved to know for a fact that I hadn't become attached to all the fringe benefits of being a media darling. What was driving me was still the same as the first day I hit the streets with my lipsticks — my fascination with the creative process. Luckily, as I came out of that dark period and the business regained some footing, I learned that creativity is every bit as enduring as it is intriguing.

It is all too easy to believe that we are defined by what we do and how successful we are. But when we rely too much on results to bolster our sense of self, we are putting ourselves in a precarious situation. Results are the aspect least within our control. Where we do have control is in the effort and motivation we decide to give something. And that should be the extent of our emotional investment. The more you invest in the process and the less you invest in the outcome, the easier it will be to put yourself on the line.

HOW DO YOU DO?

"What do you do?" is usually the second or third question someone will ask you after they meet you. Have you ever tried not to ask this yourself? I warn you, it's not easy. Once, I wanted to see if I could go to a party and get to know people without having to find out what they do. I lasted about fifteen minutes before I caved.

What about you? Next time you meet someone new, see how long you can avoid the subject of what they do for a living. The less emphasis you put on the professional lives of others, the better you'll be at separating your own work from your life and sense of self.

LESSON 39: **Strive for balance**

In life, as in the stock market, the more you spread your risk, the stronger you are. If you invest too much into just one sector, you leave yourself wide open for a fall. So while balance may be considered a luxury by some, it's one luxury you can't afford to go without.

We need our work to satisfy many things. First and foremost, we need to earn enough of a living to secure our primary needs for food and shelter. Beyond that, we are also entitled to look for a level of fulfillment and esteem from what we do. But while every single one of us deserves to take some pleasure and pride in our work, all of our happiness and self-esteem cannot come from work alone.

It's easy to assume that extra effort in one area can fill up your entire life. But in my experience it doesn't. No matter how fulfilled you are with your career, that type of fulfillment won't fill every need. A good quality of life relies on some level of work-life balance. What that balance consists of depends on the individual. For most of us, the key areas we need to balance are work, family, fun, and friendship. The more even our emotional investment across the board, the more stable we feel. I realize we all know this in theory, but watch how quickly we let ourselves slip into thinking that as long as we have one thing traveling well, the rest can suffer. Operate like that for too long and you'll soon see that everything suffers, including the area that you are putting all your efforts into — which can start to strain not from lack of attention but from too much!

My Story

I told you a little bit about Poppy Industries headquarters in the converted warehouse. What I haven't mentioned is that for some time, I also lived there. I had it designed so that the front half was all office and the back half was residential. But since it was a rather open plan, the separation of the two was very vague, both physically and psychologically. The way the space was designed, you could see straight through from the office areas into my private residence. I guess it was a fitting metaphor for my life at the time, barely anything dividing the personal from the professional.

The business was in its biggest growth spurt. We were expanding into many new stores both in Australia and overseas. This was back when I had just returned from securing the launch of Poppy lipsticks in Barneys New York, and I was in constant contact with their buyers and PR department as they prepped to unveil this strange little Australian brand (and strange little Australian girl) in the coming November.

These were the days before e-mail. Remember those? (Or, if you aren't old enough, then imagine those.) The most convenient form of communication with other countries was by fax and phone. I had about six lines for the business and one private line for me. I can't tell you how many times during that period I would be awoken at 3 AM by the business line ringing. "Hello," I would croak. "Poppy is that you?" a perky, caffeinated American voice would ask. It was always someone from Barneys who had misjudged the time difference between Melbourne and New York, but I didn't mind; it was just one of the hazards of literally living at work.

Given this home and work setup, the hardest time of the day for me came around 6 PM when everyone would leave. During business hours, the offices were a hive of activity. Phones ringing, printers going, people buzzing, meetings happening, appointments arriving, and keyboards clicking. Then, suddenly after the last person had left, silence. The phones died down and everything else that whirred, beeped, or buzzed was shut down for the night. Boy, was that a brutal adjustment. In an instant, the same space had to become my home, and the difference in activity was palpable. It felt like I existed only for work hours and every thing else was just filling in time until the beginning of the next workday.

Much as I love to laze around on the couch watching TV, it's hard to feel homey when it's the same couch where appointments wait to see you and meetings take place. I would find myself sitting bolt upright and watching *The Simpsons* as if it were a PowerPoint presentation. I just couldn't relax.

Finally, I came to the conclusion that I would have to find separate living arrangements if I wanted to stay sane. I actually started to feel like Jack Nicholson in *The Shining*—"All work and nowhere to play makes Poppy a dull girl."

One of the best ways I've found to balance out my life sounds so old-fashioned, it's like something your granny may ask you about at a family function. I am almost embarrassed to suggest it, but here goes: hobbies.

That's right. Hobbies, interests, and activities that are pure fun and have absolutely nothing to do with the pursuit of any profit, networking, or career-related goal are vital to a healthy, balanced life. I make it my business to go to book groups, flea markets, knitting classes, and a whole host of other things that are completely removed from my professional life. And every aspect of my life is the better for it.

LESSON 40: **Cold-calling the easy way**

The very idea of approaching people you barely know (or don't know at all) and trying to convince them of something is frightening in and of itself. And even though I realize that the terror I feel about making a cold call is completely out of proportion to the situation, I still find that I have to talk myself into doing it.

I remind myself of the following: Everyone I know who has any success in any area has had to do some sort of cold-calling along the way. At some point they have all had to take a deep breath and just do it, make an approach. I don't know anyone who finds this comfortable, but I do know people (myself included) who have learned how to do it without a mild cardiac arrest each time.

Preparation is the one thing guaranteed to take the edge off these experiences. The more I prepare, the easier I am able to get through each cold call and the better the results. Here is my three-step method:

1. **I will survive.** The first challenge is to convince yourself that you will survive regardless of the outcome. This may sound obvious, but it is easy to get into a hyper-nervous state about the cold call and forget that the worst that can happen is that you'll have to endure the sound of the dreaded no.

2. **Plan B.** A backup plan is the risk taker's security blanket: that warm, fuzzy, and comforting feeling that while you really want something to work, you do have other options and alternatives. These alternatives may not be as good as your first preference, but acknowledging that you have other options helps enormously with nerves. Very rarely is there no backup plan. You may have to look long and hard, but you'll find them. I wait until I have a few plan Bs in mind before I make the approach to my first preference. I mentally list them just before, and have even found myself silently repeating them back in those nervous moments while waiting to see or speak to someone. When I take the time to accept that no matter how much I want something it is not the end if I don't get it, the difference in my demeanor is remarkable.

3. **Helping vs. selling.** This type of preparation involves taking the time to understand as much you can about the person, business, or organization that you are approaching. All this takes is a little investigation and observation so that when the time comes, you have a sense of what is in it for them. Imagine yourself in the role of helper instead of salesperson, and think about their needs. I find this alleviates a great deal of psychological pressure. When you are

all filled up with your own hopes, you feel like you are about to burst. But change your focus for while and think of what could be the hopes, and wants of the other, and your tension begins to deflate. You are able then to act with determination instead of desperation.

My Story

Every city has at least one very trendy neighborhood, and in Melbourne circa 1991 it was Chapel Street — a long stretch of cafés, shops, restaurants, and night-clubs. It was here that I prowled around, preparing to approach various boutiques to sell my lipsticks. This was well before my brand was known. In fact, I don't think the first production run of the lipsticks was even completed. At this point, I was just compiling a list of stores that I would attempt to sell through when the product was ready.

I decided to divide them into three tiers according to preference. My allocations were based on a number of factors. First, the "hipness." Which were the most fashionable stores and why? Then the clientele. I would watch to see who was going in and out of these stores. Were these people my market? Then the mer-chandise. Was the clothing appropriate? Was it too dressy or too casual? What about the price points? Would lipsticks seem too small among very expensive things? How about the decor? Would the look of my brand be at odds with the rest of the store? After examining these and other factors, I was able to get a sense of which stores would be the best, pretty good, or all wrong.

One clear front-runner emerged. This store's clothes and designer received a great deal of fashion press. The styles ranged from casual chic to sexy evening. The mood was feminine but edgy. The prices were right and they sold other accessories like jewelry and bags, so I knew they were not averse to smaller items. While observing who was going in and out, I noticed something very interesting. Teenagers were dragging their moms in to buy them something they really wanted. You would see the mothers and daughters going in with the daughters looking pensive. On the way out, the daughter, shopping bag in hand, was usually grinning ear to ear as the mother zipped up her purse.

When it came time to call on the store's owner, I had something of an uphill battle on my hands. She had never thought about selling lipsticks before and was obviously on the fence. So, I asked her to consider it another accessory like the jewelry. I mentioned that

I had noticed many of her younger customers brought their moms in to show them something. I suggested that the lipstick might be something that both mother and daughter could take an interest in, as there were colors for all ages. "I know it isn't a high price purchase for you, but it is a bonding experience that can add to the fun your customers have together in the store."

This may not have been the clincher, but it certainly helped. She appreciated that I was aware of her customers and was looking at ways for her customers to enjoy shopping in the store. In the end, we agreed that she would take the lipsticks on a trial basis. I wanted this store the most out of all of them, so I was willing to be flexible with the terms. As it turned out, she sold through her entire first order within about ten days and I didn't need to do any more convincing. The lipsticks had already done that all by themselves.

Without cold-calling, you're guaranteed to miss out. Of course, to reap the benefits, you have to be prepared. The better prepared you are, the better your chances. As you can see by my example, your prep work doesn't need to be complicated, expertly crafted, or sophisticated, nor do you need anyone else to help you with it. The best preparation comes from taking the time to:

- Manage your own feelings and expectations
- Figure out what backup options exist
- Learn about your intended target

Being prepared helps to polish your presentation and protects you from many of the nerves that come with cold-calling. Although it still may not feel like a walk in the park, you can rest assured that it is a well-trodden path on which many successful people have walked.

LESSON 41: Get rocks in your head

You probably don't need me to tell you that many people—perhaps you among them—are terrified of public speaking. Oftentimes, it is the people that you would not expect to be scared, the ones who are extremely confident in other areas, whose knees turn to jelly at the thought of speaking in front of an audience. Yet many careers rely increasingly on being able to get up in front of others and orate. So how are you to do this if it doesn't come naturally?

At one point, I was doing an enormous amount of public speaking. There were years when I was giving a speech or two every month. When I realized that public speaking was becoming a large part of my role, I considered getting some training, but ultimately decided against it.

The reason for my decision was this: I noticed that the speakers who really made an impact on me were not necessarily the most smooth and professional. In fact, the flawless wonders were the ones who could actually make me drift off. The speakers that got my attention tended to be the more natural ones. Not so natural that they were flustered and all over the place, mind you, but natural enough to still seem real. Occasionally they may trip up, but no one minds because it feels so much more intimate. One political commentator's assessment of George W. Bush's and Al Gore's performances during the 2000 TV debates explains the difference to a tee: "Bush could speak to an auditorium and make you feel you were in his living room, whereas Gore could speak in his living room and make you feel you are in an auditorium." Sometimes too much polish can lack connection regardless of how relevant or smart your message is.

So how do you find that effective middle ground where you are confident but still personable? I suggest you get rocks in your head—identify a few "thought rocks," or words that sum up what you are trying to get across, and grab on to them as soon as you begin to feel a little flooded. While memorizing sentences can sound rote, I found that memorizing three or four "thought rocks" in the shape of words helped me focus without curtailing my freedom of expression.

For instance, I would always get very nervous before meeting with buyers for department stores and big accounts for the first time. The "rocks" I used to keep me from wandering too far away from my strongest pitch points were "innovation," "spirit" and "specialty." Those were what I identified as my brand's strongest selling points. So any time I felt lost at sea with the conversation, I thought of those words and gently brought my pitch back toward anything that could support those words.

The beauty of this method is it allows security and spontaneity to coexist. Ultimately, it's not a flawless performance but your comfort level that makes for a compelling presentation. When you are comfortable with yourself, the audience is comfortable with you — so it helps to figure out any way to relax before the presentation.

My Story

It wasn't until I was on the plane that I realized it was a big deal to have been named Young Australian of the Year. It was the end of 1994, and I was on my way back from a business trip in New York thinking about the call I'd received a couple of days ago in my hotel room. An Australian official rang to inform me that the council in charge of deciding national honors had voted me Young Australian of the Year for the coming year of 1995.

"Would you accept the award?" he asked.

"Um . . . yes. Thank you," I said, slightly confused. At that moment, Australia and this award were literally a world away.

On my way back over the Pacific, it began to dawn on me that this was a very prestigious award. So prestigious, in fact, that I started to wonder whether I deserved it and whether I should accept it for just starting a lipstick business. I had a very long flight to mull it over. By the time I got home, I had decided to accept because my business did show other young Australians that we had a country blessed with a great deal of opportunity, and I was pretty damned flattered.

A month or so later, a car came to drive me to the ceremony. On the way there, we were actually accompanied by a police escort! At the ceremony, the prime minister of Australia officially handed the awards to both the Australian of the Year and the Young Australian of the Year.

Prior to this award I had been giving speeches to schools, business organizations, and women's networking groups. Sometimes I was really "on" and it came off great, and other times I was more flat. But I never accepted any payment for these and would only do them if I felt some connection with the suggested audience. I tried not to put myself under too much pressure. It may sound corny, but this was my way of giving back a little by trying to inspire others.

Now that I had been given this award, it was a whole different ball game. Every year, the award recipient was booked on a national speaking tour organized by the council. Throughout 1995, I was to give at least one speech in every city and state in Australia. As to when, why, where, and to whom, that was now out of my hands and up to the council to decide.

This time I was speaking as Young Australian of the Year and not as Poppy King. Often, I felt very out of place and incredibly superficial, especially when I had to explain my story to groups of Aboriginals for whom lipstick is about as high up on the priorities list as pink elephants.

The most baffling speech I ever gave, however, was at a conference of local councilmen in Western Australia—known as the Wild West for a reason. This was a conference of men in local government positions and, as some light relief, the Young Australian of the Year was traditionally a guest at this annual event. Usually this honor was bestowed on a famous athlete. This year it happened to be not only a girl, but a girl in the lipstick business.

You would have to launch me into outer space to get me in front of an audience more alien: middle-aged men who considered deodorant a cosmetic and not a necessity. I don't think I have ever felt more awkward in my entire life. There must have been at least a hundred of them out there in the auditorium, struggling to understand the difference between matte and glossy lipstick.

I was so relieved when my speech was over. Thinking of my audience naked would definitely not have helped me get through this one. I wish I could say the same for them. I shudder to think what they may have been picturing.

No amount of time, comfort, or practice can insure you against the normal slipups and glitches that go with public speaking and presentations. But it does get easier the more you do it. The ease comes from knowing that all you can do on any given day is your best. So just focus on the main points, those "rocks" that you're trying to get across, then relax and forget about yourself.

It's not as much about you as what you have to say, and we all have a lot to share in that department.

LESSON 42: Hierarchies are everywhere

When I was younger, I thought that the only time I would come face-to-face with rank would be if I joined the army. As it turns out, the civilian world can be as subject to rank as military forces. At times it is subtle and other times very clear. Titles such as "VP of marketing," "director," or "general manager" are obvious, but even in the absence of titles, human beings are adept at sniffing out a hierarchy. As soon as you put two or more people together, some kind of power structure ensues.

When pursuing ideas, following dreams, or furthering careers, we all have to rely on other people's decision making authority somewhere along the way. While you can't avoid it, neither should you agonize over it. Remember authority figures are as human as you are. While the getting or losing of authority is what tends to preoccupy us most, the real cause for concern are the assumptions surrounding authority—jumping to the conclusion that someone is in authority because they know everything and are perfect or, alternatively, that they know nothing and have just lucked into that position. If I don't watch myself I can make that judgment in the first meeting, and settle comfortably into it unless the need to revise it is made painstakingly clear.

In the end, I have never come across someone in an authority position who is devoid of any skill and has nothing that I can learn from. Their skills and talents may not be immediately apparent; they may not even be talents you admire. But anyone who has maintained a level of success can stay there only if they have something to offer.

My Story

Back in the days when I was running all over the place
to get some more funding into the business, I got what
I thought was a very promising appointment with a
very senior person at a huge, international cosmetics company. The meeting had come about through
a whole chain of connections. Someone I knew knew
someone who knew someone who knew someone, and
so on. I never actually spoke to the person who set
this up, as it all came down the line like a game of
telephone.

I didn't ask any questions. All I knew was that I
had an audience with a powerful person in my industry. And he sure did look and sound the part. He
had a French accent and was exquisitely put together.
His skin, fingernails, even his hair, was immaculately
groomed. In fact, the second I laid eyes on him, I felt
very messy.

I had brought some coworkers to help me with the
investment pitch. I did my part, explaining where,
how, and why the brand had come into being. He asked
a few questions and looked politely through some of
our branding materials. As I finished up and the others got ready to begin their part of the pitch, they suddenly found they couldn't get a word in edgewise. In

that brief pause, our host had gone from passive to somewhat aggressive, giving us a raft of opinion on what we had done right, what we had done wrong, where the weaknesses were, what we needed to look out for, and what problems lay ahead. When my side of the table became red-faced, defensive, and argumentative, things became very awkward.

I felt crestfallen—not just about the meeting but our entire future. While I had been dismissed in these types of meetings before, I had never been utterly dissected. When it was time to go, I felt absurd as I extended my hand for the obligatory handshake. All of us, including the guy we had come to see, looked like we had just walked through a minefield.

What an idiot, we all agreed on the way out. "He was so full of — —," one of my associates said. "What would he know about marketing anything these days? He was so old school. How about the look of him? How pompous."

Human nature often goes to this place when hurt or offended, a place of attack, and attack we did. How the heck does such an idiot end up in a position like that? we all pondered.

Still smarting a few weeks later, I managed to get some information that shed a little light on that meeting and why it had been so off-key. As it turned out, the reasons why we thought we were there and the reasons why the senior executive thought we were there were very different. He had agreed to the meeting as a favor to a friend and was under the impression that all we wanted was some advice. No wonder he just cut it short straight after my spiel. I cringed just thinking about it, not only when I first found out but for years thereafter.

Five or so years later, and in a completely different country, I had a meeting with the same corporation, but with someone even higher up this time and in control of a much bigger market. When I walked into this person's office, I couldn't help noticing the incredible view first. Then I noted how familiar my host looked. It was him! The same guy. My face went as red as my lipstick as he said, "We met some time back."

The door had been closed by his assistant, so I was trapped. "I know that meeting didn't go very well and I apologize," I said. I figured confessing was my best option. This time, we ended up having a great meeting and I got the chance to see him in a completely different context. Now, there was no question in my mind as to why he was in such a powerful position. Let's face it . . . Anyone who can get their hair that perfect has got to know something that I don't!

Wheeling and dealing with authority is a lifelong process. I have to admit, I was never all that good at having authority. I just assumed that being the Poppy of a
company called Poppy Industries was proof enough, and
that everyone working for me would simply respect my
leadership role and fall in line accordingly. While this
laissez-faire approach was fine by some of the wonderful
people with whom I worked, there were also those who
undermined me and took advantage of the fact that I was
squeamish about my position.

Over the years, I've grown to understand the role of
authority a lot better and am no longer overwhelmed by
my own or that of others. The bottom line is that when
we have authority we have a responsibility to live up to
it, and when we come across authority we have a responsibility to resist hasty judgments of any extreme, good or
bad.

SCIENTIFIC PROOF: THE DANGER
OF ASSUMPTIONS

Learning to keep an open mind helped me better understand and deal with authority. And by open mind, I mean not assuming that people in authority—whether it's me or someone else—are always right or always wrong.

Psychological studies with rats confirm that preconceived notions lead to a lack of movement. In a famous experiment, three rats were placed in three different cages. Each cage had levers that activated the delivery of food pellets. The first rat got a pellet every time he pressed the lever. This rat got very bored quickly. The second rat never got a pellet no matter how many times he pressed. This rat became depressed and despondent. The third rat got a pellet only some of the time; he could never assume what was going to happen. That rat became highly active.

Authority is just like pressing that lever. When you assume it will always be the same you will not be at your best. But staying away from any one assumption, be it positive or negative, will ensure that you're constantly surprised and invigorated. This can help you find the strengths in other people and yourself.

LESSON 43: The ABC of business: Always be courteous

I make it a rule not to save my politeness for the people and situations that "matter." Beyond the fact that all people deserve respect, being nice across the board is just sound career practice. There are so many little things you can do to make yourself stand out from the pack. Sending a thank-you note, delivering on a nonessential promise, returning an e-mail, even something as basic as letting people finish their sentences and looking them in the eye while you're speaking . . . These type of things don't require a great deal of effort and can reap tremendous rewards, and yet many people often consider them a waste of energy.

Since courtesy is not practiced as much as you would hope, making it a habit will give you an edge on the competition. One of the nicest things anyone ever said to me was when they were thanking me for a lipstick I had sent. She was a maître d' at a restaurant, and after noticing her look and demeanor, I told her that she'd be a great advertisement and I would send her one of my lipsticks. I included my card along with the lipstick, and when she called to thank me she said that she knew I would be a big success because "so many people trying to promote things promise to send me this or that, but only three —

you included — have actually ever followed through. You
obviously have what it takes."

It isn't always easy to quantify or articulate exactly
what you can gain out of doing the little things. Your
good gesture may be ignored or it may be thoughtfully
noted. You never know — but as history has shown, none
of us are as smart as we think we are when it comes to
predicting what will or won't have an impact on our lives.
Sometimes, the smallest, least significant interactions can
have the most weighty and meaningful consequences.

My Story

When I was looking high and low for investors, I
milked every bit of drama that I possibly could out of
those experiences that I decided were going to alter
my destiny. The next meeting was always going to be
the one that would catapult the business to legendary
success.

On the day of the big meeting, I would wake up
early in the morning, look at the sky, and think, This
is the day. As I brushed my teeth, I would look at my
reflection and think, Today you are struggling, but tomorrow everything will be different!

In the entire twelve years of Poppy Industries, not
one of the meetings or interactions that I had thought
would be "life changing" ever were. Not one of them!

In fact, all the biggest changes, twists, and turns came from places and people I never expected.

The meeting that ended up having the biggest, most amazing impact, the one that ended up changing absolutely everything for me in every single way, including the country I live in and what I am doing right this very moment, was just a run-of-the-mill "deskside" with a magazine beauty editor. Anytime I had a new product to show, I would schedule these desksides, a series of fifteen-minute meetings with different magazine editors. You show them the product, give a little explanation, and then leave. Often you do about ten of them a day. The most I ever thought I could get from this was an editorial mention of my latest product.

A couple of years subsequent to our meeting, that editor left her position to rejoin the cosmetics industry, where she had started her career. In 2002, approximately three years after our routine little meeting, this former editor was sitting across the desk from her boss and being asked a question about whom they should hire for something.

"Poppy King," she responded.

Although I was half a world away and had no idea I was being discussed, at that moment my life changed forever. As for what happened next, that is a whole other book.

I am still processing how a simple twist of fate set me on a path that led me to a whole new set of dreams. Never in a million years would I have known that that one meeting would have such far-reaching results. Which just goes to show, you never can tell where that twist could come from, so maximize your opportunities by making courtesy, charm, politeness, and general niceness a regular way of being. Yes, it will take a little effort and energy on your part, but take my word, the results are more than worth the trouble.

Conclusion

Rejection, monetary loss, mistakes, embarrassment, and misunderstanding are just some of the things we fear as we strive for any personal or professional expansion. But these can only hurt us insofar as they hurt our idea of ourselves. Your sense of self can never be entirely inured to the bumps on the road—everyone's ego, pride, and self-respect take a beating once in a while. But no matter how much you may get knocked about by the hands of fate, ultimately, the way you feel about yourself depends only on you, not on what happens to you.

How do you feel about yourself when you lie down at night? Are you satisfied that your efforts, goals, and actions are consistent with your values? The more you can accept yourself, the less you have to fear from the outside world when you're putting yourself on the line. Toward that end, here is a short recap of the advice I've provided in this chapter:

- **Balance is essential.** You are not your job. But how would you know that if all you ever did was sit in your office? Making relationships and outside interests a priority will serve to remind you that there is more to life than business alone.

- **Prepare to cold-call.** To make the most out of every cold call, you have to be in the right frame of mind. Use the three-step method I've developed to ensure that your efforts don't go unrewarded.

- **Engage your audience.** Whether you're giving a boardroom presentation or addressing an audience of hundreds, being too polished can be a liability. Connect to your audience by leaving room for spontaneity in your speech, and avoid becoming self-conscious by reminding yourself that it's not about you but what you have to say.

- **Authority isn't personal.** Dealing with authority figures isn't easy. Nor can you breeze through life as an authority figure yourself. Watch what you assume about those in authority, and once you get some authority of your own, make sure you don't let it go to your head.

- **Get ahead the easy way.** Let others overlook the niceties and courtesies. If you go out of your way to be pleasant and polite every chance you get, you just may find yourself landing one lucky break after another.

Writing this book has been one of my main goals for quite some time, but only recently did I muster the courage to actually go through with it. That isn't to say that I don't still have moments when I am more than a little terrified by the whole thing. In fact, it was during one of those moments a little while ago that I decided to move away from my computer and take a TV break. Flipping through the channels, I found an old black-and-white film to watch — and not a moment too soon.

The lead actress said something so appropriate that it quieted my fear of judgment and inspired me to get back to the computer and keep on writing. She turned to her costar and said, "Remember that all the water in the seven seas can only sink a ship if it gets inside." She's right. The only time any outside opinion or event can truly knock you down is if you let it get inside.

9

THE GREATEST SHOW

ON EARTH

WHEN I WAS still a young girl, my mom would sometimes leave me to wait in the car while she ran her errands. To pass the time, I often sang along to her tape of the musical *Evita*. By the time she got back, I would have already married a dignitary; fallen in love with a handsome freedom fighter; become the most famous woman in the land, then a hated one; and, ultimately, died a tragic death. Evita and I were both so misunderstood! In her case, it was an entire nation that didn't understand. In mine, it was a schoolyard. But at ten, the difference between the two wasn't all that clear, so, yes, Evita and I were one and the same!

Since no one told me that life wasn't meant to be lived with the drama and massive exaggeration of a Broadway musical, I had no clue that the stage and everyday life have very little in common. No wonder the media and I had such a long-lasting love affair in the beginning—we both have a flair for the dramatic.

Without drama, there is nothing for the media to report. But just as drama alone won't make your business a success, neither will the media. You need more than that to make it, because while the media can get you attention, it cannot guarantee success. Attention to your product, your service, your business, your ideas, and attention to you. While all this is extremely valuable and sought after, it is not the answer. To set out to do something on the assumption that the media will carry the bulk of the load is just asking for trouble. The weight of any plan, business or otherwise, needs to be carried by something much more substantive.

That said, there's no denying the power of the media when it comes to raising consumer awareness of you or a product. And there's no denying the power of drama to raise the media's awareness. Having dealt with the press my entire adult life, I hope I can help you better understand the media by sharing my thoughts and experiences.

My Story

Having always thought of myself as an animated person, I was surprised when cameramen, producers, and

the like would stop the take and urge me to give it even more expression. Eventually, after I had been on television numerous times, I got the routine down. I knew that I had to exaggerate everything so as not to look wooden. Despite feeling ridiculous every time I did it, I managed.

But even after years of practice, I learned the media could still surprise me. A girl I knew socially had her own successful TV show. She was a real character, a very bold, unconventional, no-fear type — and funny. I liked her and was happy to go on her talk show as a guest. I expected the unexpected but I hadn't quite anticipated this: She had decided that we should do the interview in my hotel room in Sydney . . . and on the bed!

She was a hard person to say no to, and seeing as it was her show after all, I agreed. As soon as the cameras were rolling, I was already uncomfortable because every position I assumed on the bed felt either unnatural or porn-starish. I ended up in a rather stiff and pious pose, completely out of keeping with the casual tone of the interview.

She asked some pretty wacky questions and I tried to go along with it as best I could without appearing like I had a pole up my you-know-what. The challenge increased tenfold when she suddenly decided to start jumping up and down on the bed and invited me to do the same. At that moment I was faced with a terrible dilemma. I am not the jump-on-the-bed type, and I wasn't even dressed appropriately for the activity. So either I could refuse and come across as someone with no sense of fun, or I could do it even though I was going to be way out of my element.

Hoping that what feels foolish to do on TV won't look as foolish to watch, I got up and joined in. I can't remember what I ended up looking like on that show. Come to think of it, I can't remember what I looked like on most of the TV shows I was on. More often than not, I couldn't bring myself to actually look at the screen when I was on TV. I watched my entire *60 Minutes* interview in what my friend described as "crash position"—head between my knees, hands and elbows around my ears, and my eyes shut tight. My sole comfort was knowing that both my reaction to my own media and my actions in the media were exaggerated and not at all what I am like in real life.

While I have both an extroverted and an introverted side, the media has no use for the latter. The meek may inherit the earth but they won't get on television. In terms of facial and vocal expression, what seems natural in real life comes across completely flat on TV, and what seems natural on TV comes across as insane behavior in real life.

The media relies on exaggeration, taking small things and magnifying them hundreds of times over. That's why when someone sees a celebrity in the flesh the first thing they will say is that the person is much smaller than they appear on screen. Of course, the media can't do it all alone, without some help from its subject. That's where you and I come in—we have to give them something dramatic to work with.

LESSON 44: Local girl makes headline

Most of the editors I know would much rather get a press release and a follow-up phone call than have to go to some fancy event, cooked up by a PR company at considerable expense to their client (aka you), to get the exact same information. While fun press events can't hurt when there's plenty of money to throw around, they are by no means essential to getting through to the media. What is essential is a strong press release—and that doesn't have to be difficult, nor cost much more than a little time and imagination. Here are the four main ingredients of a solid press release:

1. **Lead with the headline.** The best way to approach the media is headline first. There is a rather alarming sta-

tistic that tells you the average amount of text people read after reading the headline. It is very small, maybe two paragraphs max. The headline is the most important factor. It's your hook. The more the media can see a headline that could accompany your story, the more interest they will take. So before you do anything, make sure there is a clear hook somewhere in your information. A hook performs the same function in the PR world as in the fishing world; it reels something in. To be successful, your hook needs to be sharp and tantalizing. Something in your story must be different. This is how someone once summed it up for me: "Dog bites man" is not an interesting headline, but "Man bites dog" is more like it.

2. **Make sure it's relevant.** Not only do you have to have a headline, but your headline must be catchy. As for what constitutes catchy, well, that depends entirely on the nature of the media you are approaching and their audience. For example, *Vogue*'s idea of catchy will be different than the *National Enquirer*'s. While only one of them is going to be interested in an Elvis sighting (unless, of course, Elvis was seen in the front row of an Armani Privé runway show), both *Vogue* and the *Enquirer* will need some kind of hook. Tailor it to the publication or media outlet.

3. **Get excited!** The secret to being newsworthy is not so much *what* you have to say but *how* you say it. Language is what can make all the difference to success with media communication. To find a language that works, I invite you to enter the world of the superhero. There is a lot that can be learned from the concise, powerful, informative, and exciting language found in comic books. It may be simple but it is by no means stupid. "Faster than a speeding bullet, more powerful than a locomotive, and able to leap tall buildings in a single bound" is a great example of a sentence that imparts information in a manner that is clear, strong, and intriguing. You get it. You get that this Superman has special powers, and those powers are explained and demonstrated in just one sentence. If only every press release could be this good.

4. **Who, what, where, why, and how.** The biggest villain in press release writing is too much fluffy unnecessary stuff and not enough factual information about what it is, where to get it, how much it costs, and who is behind it. That's what the media people want to know. The first thing any reporter learns in school is: Every story must answer the five questions: Who? What? Where? Why? How? So think like a jour-

nalist and make sure your press release delivers the key information.

My Story

I knew I was in trouble the second he started walking toward me. He had been giving me the eye for a while and now he was coming over.

"This is not a library, young lady," the guy at the magazine store said. "Are you planning on buying any of these?"

Annoying as he was, he was right. I had been in this magazine store for a while opening all the fashion magazines to the editor's page and writing down the name of each beauty editor in my notebook. I could have done this at the library, but I got lazy and just went to the local store instead. It was only a couple of months before my lipsticks were to go on sale and I wanted to get some information about them to the magazines and other press. By this stage, I had found out through people in the fashion industry that the usual procedure was to send a press release about the product to the relevant editor. It occurred to me that finding out the name of these editors would be very easy. They're right there on the masthead at the front of the magazine.

So that is what I did, and as soon as I had my names and addresses, I set about preparing what it was I wanted to send them. And more important, what it was I wanted to say. As I was not long out of school I had no experience in the world of PR and no budget to pay someone who did, so for direction I thought about the type of messages I saw in the media and how I could tailor mine to have the same impact. This wasn't the time to reinvent the wheel, but instead to look at what was already making that wheel turn and see what I could add to that motion. Gillette razors came to mind.

Now you may wonder what men's shaving has to do with lipstick, but for years the advertisements for Gillette had featured some gray-haired, old guy proclaiming: "I liked the razors so much, I bought the company." Obviously the advertising agency thought this message was strong enough to build an entire campaign around. Big companies pay thousands of dollars in research before they go to market with their messages, and little guys like us can benefit from this without laying out a cent. All we have to do is take notice of what these big companies have decided works and then figure out how we can do something similar but say it differently.

Credibility was what Gillette was aiming for with their message, a credibility that comes with the statement that their products are so good, they were reason

enough for someone to buy the entire business. Using this as a springboard, I found the message I wanted to send to the media:

"I couldn't find a lipstick I wanted so I started my own company."

That was the heading on my press release. I, too, could demonstrate the kind of credibility that comes from someone who believes so much in their product, they stand behind the entire company.

I could see this statement as a headline. It had the simple, powerful heroics that the media loves. In my case the heroics were the feat of starting a company. A good press release can find the heroics in anything from a person to a product, and they are there if you look hard enough.

Heroes and villains. Good and bad. Victory and defeat. The media deals in black and white, and if you want to get their attention so should you. What are the most obviously compelling aspects of what you are trying to say or sell? Even the most enthusiastic editors do not have the time or desire to sift through piles of text to get to the crux of a press release. But if you can take your information and turn it into a series of great captions or blurbs like you'd find in a colorful and exciting comic strip, you will be amazed to find that what seems like a huge wall between the little guy and the media can be leapt over in a single bound.

WRITE YOUR OWN PRESS RELEASE

Once you have the format down, writing your company's press release should be fun. Think of it as your chance to finally put your pitch into words. To give you a sense of how it's done, take a look at a recent press release put out by yours truly:

Lipstick Queen—Media Release

Everyone is talking about the return of lipstick after years of lip gloss . . . but for some . . . lipstick never left center stage. *(This first paragraph gives the headline—THE RETURN OF LIPSTICK!)*

One such person is Poppy King, who at the age of seven became so obsessed with lipstick as soon as she graduated high school . . . she started her own lipstick brand! *(Here, I establish my credibility and pique curiosity.)*

Born in Melbourne, Australia, but now a resident of New York City, her career in lipstick is legendary and she is known all over the world as a bona fide lipstick queen. *(I answer the question of who I am.)*

Hence the name of her new brand and her return to her own lipstick line after spending three years working in a large cosmetics corporation. *(I say why I'm doing it.)*

LIPSTICK QUEEN is as simple as it is sensational. Poppy has

designed her ultimate 10 shades and each shade comes in two strengths … sheer or opaque. You get to choose whether you like the shade with just a hint of color or whether you want full-blown intense coverage. *(I tell you what it is.)*

But that's not all … you also get to choose if you want to be a SAINT or a SINNER … that's right!! The sheer lipsticks are the SAINTS and the opaque are the SINNERS. *(I throw in personality and a point of differentiation.)*

Explore all sides of your personality with these beautiful and chic lipsticks which are non-drying, long lasting and so gorgeous on they could only come from someone obsessed with perfect lip color. *(Explaining the benefits.)*

LIPSTICK QUEENS unite! This line is for us … whether you never left or are returning once again to lipstick … there is nothing as glamorous as the look, the feel and the experience of wonderful lipstick. *(The heroics! And a call to action.)*

Available at Barneys New York and the other great stores listed on www.lipstickqueen.com

RRP $18 in the USA *(Vital information on where to get it and for how much.)*

For more information please contact *XXX* at *XXXX* *(How and who to contact—also crucial information.)*

And there you have it, a full-length, entirely professional press release. Now that doesn't look all that complicated, does it?

LESSON 45: **Timing is everything**

Think of the media as a speeding train—once it gets on a certain track it will zoom along that track so decidedly and so quickly that nothing, not even the truth, can stand in its way. Even the best publicists in the world cannot control the media—when it runs with something it runs, and when it doesn't it doesn't. There are no guarantees as to what will or won't get traction, but a lot depends on being in the right place at the right time.

People will try to convince you otherwise. Entire industries and professions have been built on being able to provide the false comfort that they know how to master the media when in truth, no one does. What these people do know is how to manage it—a far more realistic goal. If you learn how to manage the parts you do have control over, you are much more likely to get good results from the parts you can't control. For instance, while you cannot control what will or won't get attention from the media, you can control the timing of when you seek that attention.

There are good, bad, and even better times to start your media efforts. After all, if your efforts work and you do manage to get some attention, you'll find yourself in hot water if you're not ready for the attention. Out of the two scenarios, lack of attention from the media and attention at the wrong time, the latter can be decidedly more dangerous.

The best time to make an approach is when you have enough of an infrastructure, or a foundation, to make use of any attention. In other words, you need to have your ducks in a row so that if the media does bring you attention and opportunities, all the systems you need to capitalize on the interest are in place.

Thinking you can ask outsiders to wait while you get your act together? Think again. If you make a promise and can't deliver, people will just move on. So before you make any moves, before you send off that first press release, ask yourself (or your publicist), Can I deliver on this promise? I suggest you delay your media gratification until you can be sure that you can give instant gratification to the media's viewers, readers, listeners, and users. People make the decision to buy or take an interest in an instant when they read, see, or hear something. If you're not ready to fulfill their wish pronto, the impulse will have passed and so will have your opportunity.

My Story

Back in 1993 you couldn't ask for a better vehicle than Barneys when it came to public relations. They were at the center of everything chic, and any brand they endorsed was of immediate interest. It was a few months before their flagship Madison Avenue store was about to open, and with all the anticipation surrounding the grand opening, you would have thought it was Willy Wonka opening his chocolate factory for the first time.

On this particular day, the people with the golden tickets were the beauty editors who had been invited to experience the hot new brands that Barneys had scoured the world to find. In a large, sunny room on the top floor of the Barneys offices sat me and three other vendors. Behind each of us was a display of our products for the editors to touch and feel as they moved around the room. Over a period of two days, editor after editor poured in. It was an opportunity of a lifetime for a nineteen-year-old kid like me who would never have been able to get this caliber of audience without the Barneys touch.

Many of the editors who came during that event brought along their assistants. Those editors have since left and most of the assistants that I met back then have now been promoted and are running the magazines. One of the young girls who came along and interviewed me has become a very powerful and influential person in the fashion/beauty world. After she saw the lipsticks at the Barneys preview, we went for coffee and she pulled out a tape recorder, explaining that her boss had asked her to write a paragraph on me for an upcoming issue of *Vogue*.

We chatted away for a while about the brand and how and why I started it. That paragraph ended up being a full-page article with a huge photo. Do you know the thousands of dollars it costs for a full-page ad in American *Vogue*? Something like $40,000 or more. And this was the fall issue, which is the biggest and most widely read. An advertisement is one thing, but a full page of editorial and the credibility that it lends the subject is priceless.

Many years later, I found out that the head of one of the biggest cosmetics corporations in the world tore out that page on me and brought it to a meeting of his senior executives to tell them they'd better get their creativity going to compete with people like me. Me! Strange, weird little me from half a world away!

As a result of *Vogue*'s attention, the offers, interviews, and interest poured in. This was just before the cusp of the indie explosion in everything from cosmetics to films to ice cream, and people wanted to know more about someone starting their own brand. America was fascinated with upstarts. But here's the thing . . . I didn't live in America. I lived in Australia. My business in Australia was growing by leaps and bounds, so I needed to get that organized before I could focus on the United States.

So I said, "Thank you, New York. I am so glad you want to hear more, but hold that thought and I'll get back to you when I am ready." I didn't actually say that, of course, but that is what I thought would happen. I thought I could just hit pause with the media and come back later to get it started again.

By the time I did get back to New York and had enough systems and infrastructure in place to feel more able to deliver, it was too late. A wave had broken and many new hip indie brands had come onto the market. Whereas I had been one of the first to enter the race, I was now running last. I hadn't been ready for the U.S. spotlight, while others were—and once it moves on, it is almost impossible to get it back.

The media is a living, breathing organism—except that it uses information instead of oxygen to survive. If the media cannot readily get information or access to you, your product, or your business the moment its interest is piqued, the interest will disappear. If you are not able to deliver these most basic elements to the media, it usually follows that you are also not ready to deliver to their audience. So before you approach the media, check to see if the time is right for you, for them, and for the viewer.

LESSON 46: **Ask not what the media can do for you, but what you can do for . . .**

There are some things that are undeniably sacred. And while a good book on the beach and a huge Sunday breakfast are high up on that list, the media is not a sacred service. And yet, for some reason, I still get a shock any time the media blatantly behaves like a business instead of a public institution. After all, it's common knowledge that newspapers, magazines, televisions, and computer screens rely on customers to part not just with their time and attention but their money as well. The media has to make money. The higher the ratings, circulation, and page views, the more they can charge for advertising. In many ways, the media is as much a commodity as lipsticks, so it is subject to the same basic principles of supply and demand as any other business. It has to supply something targeted toward demand.

The media has to tailor their coverage, their product, to their audience. Every single day they need to come up with news, information, and entertainment to keep people tuning in, logging on, or picking up. It is a lot of pressure and they can't do it alone. Guess what, guys? As it turns out, they need us too!

The media relies on us to create the information that makes it sell. People and all their amazing, exasperating, mind-boggling, inspirational, aspirational, irrational, inventive, repetitive, and sometimes deceptive antics—that is the stuff that fills the airwaves, screens, and pages. Media coverage may be of service to you, your business, your career, or your idea, but never forget that you are also doing the media a service by providing them with something to cover.

My Story

Can you believe it? There is something in Australia called the "Tall Poppy syndrome." This refers to a uniquely Australian tendency to criticize people if they become too successful and start appearing arrogant or grandiose, a mind-set that is often contrasted with that of the United States, which seems much more supportive of people taking risks, accumulating success, and standing out from the crowd. So being named Poppy made for easy headlines when I became a well-known Australian identity and business person.

For a long time all the headlines were glowing. *"Poppy Blooms!" "Australia's Very Own Tall Poppy!"* You get the picture. I couldn't have been placed on a higher pedestal. For reasons that had little to do with any skill or talent of my own and everything to do with the media's agenda to promote me as a symbol of Australian innovation, I became the poster girl for entrepreneurial success.

Amid this amazing national acclaim, I worked to maintain my integrity. I really tried to treat all this praise with deference and dignity. At times, I had many offers, some of them involving pretty big dollars, to be featured on ads for feminine hygiene products, beverages, credit cards, cars, and banks. But I never agreed to do any because I decided to resist making money just by virtue of fame. Obviously my notoriety helped my business make money, but I felt that to take money for no other reason than celebrity was a sign of disrespect to the privileged position I had been given by the media. The least I could do was show my appreciation by drawing a line between promoting my own business and becoming a gun for hire.

This extended to public speaking. Despite how lucrative the speakers' circuit could be, I always waived any fee. Now, don't get me wrong. I am not asking for a medal. When I said I thought it was the least I could do, I meant it.

I also thought that refraining from making money purely from celebrity would protect me from criticism should anything go wrong. Somehow, I came to believe that the media was aware that I was doing my part. I completely disregarded that the media is a business, not a personal pact. It was going to do whatever it needed, whatever made for headlines. And since there had been so many positive stories about me, the second there was something negative to report — specifically in the dispute I was having with my business partners — the media jumped all over it. "Tall Poppy Cut Down!" "Wilted Poppy!" "The Seven Deadly Sins of Poppy King!" And so many more.

This went on for months, as every major newspaper, magazine, and television and radio show bent over backward to get the biggest, juiciest exposé that would reveal me and my success to be nothing more than a myth. Suddenly, what constituted news was no longer my successes but my failings. These attacks made for good headlines and good business for the media. My mistakes and shortcomings made for fodder that was just as good as any of my talents had been in the beginning.

During that awful time, many journalists asked me if I felt I was falling victim to the legendary Tall Poppy syndrome. But I knew this was a trap. If I answered yes, then the next day's papers would attack me for being ungrateful and feeling sorry for myself. So I always said no. I had to take my lumps, given that the media had been so nice about me for so long.

And it's true. You can't just have it go your way — sometimes, what suits you will suit the media. Other times, the opposite will happen. I realize it may be personally upsetting, but in fact, the media is about as

personal as a coin toss. So while my feelings were—
and I have to admit, still are—incredibly hurt by a lot
of what I read about myself, I know it's just business,
and as they say . . . there's no business like show business. The media is both a show and a business, and
the business part—the economics of what is going to
sell—will always drive the show.

I have to say, when it came to handling the media, there
were times I really messed it up. But as long as you know
that the media is a business and approach it as such, there
is no need for you to follow in my infamous footsteps. The
more you recognize and treat the media as a business—in
other words, as an entity that has to have something in it
for them—the better you will be at getting good business
out of it.

LESSON 47: Personality and the media

You don't need to look much further than the five most lucrative letters in the American alphabet—O, P, R, A, and
H—to see that personality is big business. The media, like
all brands of show business, thrives on personality so let
yours shine through. Just one caveat: To ensure that the
benefits don't only go their way, deliver your personality
strategically.

Personality run amok is the material many media outlets dream about, but it is a nightmare for the personality involved. A couple of words to bring this point home:
Britney Spears. The smartest way to make use of your
personality is in a very professional manner, one that is in
keeping with the message you want to get across.

We all have a personality. Even accountants, who can be
the butt of jokes like "What does an accountant use for con-
traception? His personality!" In defense of accountants everywhere, I happen to know many with great personalities
and, more often than not, a number of kids. Luckily for all
of us, there will always be people who respond to our own
unique personality traits. And the media is no exception.

As I mentioned before, many people and publicity
companies try so hard to get attention with expensive
gimmicks and fancy parties, but even in a world as superficial as the media, style doesn't necessarily triumph over
substance. In fact, in an industry so jaded by perks and
launches, it's the genuine that seems much more exotic.
So don't be afraid to be yourself, but think about what
parts of your personality will best serve your goals before
you expose yourself to the harsh glare of the spotlight.

My Story

I have spent a great deal of time pondering the answer to two questions, just in case a journalist or my

future husband happened to ask me. These questions say a lot about who you are and what is important to you, and I want to be prepared. The first question is, What are your ten favorite movies? The second is, If you could have anyone in the world over for a dinner party (dead or alive), whom would you have?

OK, so maybe they are not deep, existential, or intellectual questions, but they sure do say a lot about your perspective. Every time I think I have settled on my perfect answer I think of another film or another person. It is amazing where my head can go when I am determined to procrastinate!

While no one has ever actually asked me either question, I did come close in an interview years ago. It was for a section in one of Australia's most respected newspapers. I think the column was called "Up Close and Personal," and every week a notable or famous person was interviewed and asked a series of offbeat questions. When I got the call from the journalist who wrote the column, I was very happy to do it. After years of answering somewhat repetitive questions, I knew this would be more challenging.

I was right. The interview was very spontaneous and casual. As we went through most of the questions, though, I got the feeling he was pretty jaded. He had heard it all before and was just going through the motions. He kept asking somewhat sarcastic questions about what my life was like on the A list. We came to the last question. "So, Poppy, who were you in a past life?" Meaning whom did I identify with. I am sure he was expecting me to name some fashion icon like Coco Chanel, or a mysterious femme fatale from the silent movie era such as Louise Brooks. He looked stunned when my answer came out straight from the heart, I having only pondered it for a few seconds.

"Bon Scott."

The deceased, former lead singer of AC/DC had the demeanor of a time bomb that could go off at any second. Not exactly handsome, he was known more for the incredibly tight-fitting jeans that did little to hide what looked to be a prodigious manhood. So different from the manufactured pop stars of today, this guy was the real deal. He was no nancy boy doing it for the trappings; he was what he was because he could be nothing else. Not exactly the type of person you would expect your garden-variety lipstick entrepreneur to align themselves with.

"Bon Scott," my interviewer exclaimed. "Why Bon Scott?"

"Because he wrote 'Ride On,'" I answered.

"Ride On" is a song not as heavy with metal as it is with emotion. The gritty voice and raw lyrics remind us that to be human is to be totally flawed. We all have faults, we all succumb at times to our own demons, but you just keep going, keep living, and keep doing the best you can. Or as Bon says, "Keep on riding." Unfortunately what plagued him was so destructive that his ride didn't last nearly as long as his song's message—a message that resonated deeply with me despite how unlikely the source.

At the time this interview took place, I was so well known that even the journalists themselves thought there could be no surprises left. However, being a well-known personality doesn't always mean that people know your personality well. It's up to you to decide if you are willing to let them.

Strategic. Professional. Considered. These words may sound like anathema to the idea of personality, almost too contrived to be genuine. But if you take what is genuine to your personality and mix it in with the information the media needs, then you are being all of the above. And remember, while you can add personality to the way you present information, don't make the mistake of trying to use personality as a substitute for straightforward information. Always keep in mind that information and personality are exactly what the media needs.

LESSON 48: **Media is not the answer**

The media can assist your business, career, product, plan, and reputation, but it should only be part of a strategy and not the strategy itself. Whatever your big picture goals are, the media is never the answer. It is never going to solve, fix, alleviate, or eradicate any necessity. You still need a thorough plan with or without it.

Now while Oscar Wilde may have quipped that "there is only one thing in life worse than being talked about, and that is not being talked about," I have to think he was joking. What is just as bad is being talked about when you aren't ready to be, or when you can't deliver on the talk, or when the talk is filled with misinformation. And the very, very worst thing, much worse than any of the above, is to fall for the idea that getting the media talking is all you need to be a success.

My Story

I have slept in the same bed as Michael Jackson. I am very relieved to tell you he was not in it at the time. I happened to be the next guest in the hotel suite he had just vacated. It was in Sydney at the Sheraton on the Park, a hotel I often stayed at when I had business in Sydney. They always upgraded me, and for some reason, for this particular stay they comped me the presidential suite, which was the entire top floor. I knew that Michael Jackson had just been in it because it was all over the papers the day before. He had, in fact, just gotten married in it to Debbie Rowe. All the papers had reported that the weird nuptials took place in the presidential suite at the Sheraton on the Park in Sydney and here I was in an elevator with the key to this exact suite in my hand.

I was not that thrilled about it, to tell you the truth. Had it been anyone other than Michael Jackson, I might have been, but it felt creepy just opening the door and peering in at this palatial spread. The suite had many rooms including an enormous lounge area with a baby grand piano. It was so big that I seemed very little—especially when I went into the master bathroom and saw what looked to be the world's largest bathtub. The enormous marble grotto was raised up in the center of the room with a stunning view across Sydney's Centennial Park. Despite the hotel's amazing housekeeping staff, I was way too weirded out to use the same washing facilities as the previous guest, so I sidestepped the master bath in favor of one of the smaller ones.

I did not, however, forgo the patio-style balcony that stretched around the whole suite. I had never seen such a beautiful 360-degree view of Sydney. As I surveyed the sights, I realized that I was seeing Sydney from one of its highest points at the lowest point in my career. It was during the media storm surrounding the collapse of my business partnership. The possibility that my business would collapse as a result loomed ominously over the horizon. At that very moment, among all the splendor of a who-knows-how-many-thousands-of-dollars-a-night room I had been given as an upgrade, I was on the edge of possibly losing everything, of not having a cent to my name. My business, my house in Melbourne, my car . . . everything. Throughout my time with the business and the ebbs and flows of millions of dollars that had come and gone through it, I had never paid myself a great deal nor spent or saved a great deal personally, so if I lost the business, all my assets went with it. One of my biggest assets was already gone . . . my reputation.

All this media attention felt utterly chaotic. At the time, I really didn't know what I was doing with the media and why I was doing it. All I knew was that the cat had been let out of the bag, and more and more media just kept on coming. The press was not the answer to my business problems. An adviser of mine at the time had assumed it would be, and decided to try to use the media to fight what should have been a private battle. He got a nasty shock when the plan backfired. Instead of standing by their media darling of years, the media turned on me, making it clear that it does not fight battles on request unless it has its own reason to.

There is no sanctuary in attention unless you know what you are doing with it. I don't think I have ever felt less safe than the night I spent in one of the most glamorous and expensive hotel rooms in the Southern Hemisphere. If media attention was all it took to have an advantage, then I should have felt like the queen of the world. The media was so fixated on me that I was still famous enough to get an upgrade at a hotel. But so what? I tossed and turned that night on the very top floor of a very fancy hotel, whilst underneath me was nothing but thin air.

The media can be many things to a business—a launching pad, a billboard, a springboard—but it will never ever be a safety net. It's just as Evita sings in "Don't Cry for Me, Argentina": "And as for fortune and as for fame . . . They are illusions, they're not the solutions they promise to be." And it's true. They are not the answer. When it comes to approaching the media, the answer is to figure out what you're doing first and why, then decide whether or not the media will help.

PUBLICITY CHECKLIST

If the media isn't the answer, what is it? I've come to see it as the question. Or rather, a series of questions. For instance:

Q. Do you have an interesting headline for them?

A.

Q. Is the timing right?

A.

Q. Do you have all the information packaged, ready, and easily accessible?

A.

Q. Can you deliver on your promises?

A.

Q. Are you able to give something a little edge, a little personality?

A.

If you have all the right answers to the media's questions, then and only then will you have the confidence it takes to make a strong approach and a compelling case for your story.

Conclusion

Say what you will about the media, it is still the fastest way to get a message out to a broad audience. That is why advertisers buy it with advertising space and publicity agents vie for it with their contacts, press releases, and launch parties. There are many agencies you can hire to get your publicity—and I have used them on and off over the course of my career—but I must warn you, sometimes the "spin" they put on things isn't only on the messages they send to the media. They often put a spin on what they tell you as well!

If you decide against hiring an outside agency, know that armed with a good press release, you can become your own publicist. You have a shot with the media if you follow these steps:

- **Hook them with your headline.** Before you start writing your press release, get in the head of a reader. What kind of stuff is interesting to you? What would make you want to read more? For examples, look at the headlines that are in the media and see which ones really grab you.
- **Find a good time.** Press people want the information immediately. They don't wait. And neither does their audience, the consumers. Before you seek publicity, evaluate whether or not you'll be ready to deliver on your promises should your efforts generate much interest.
- **Anticipate their needs.** The media is in the business of making money. Their goal is not to broadcast your accomplishments so that people will pay attention

to you; their goal is to get people to pay attention to them. You and the media can both win if you give them something they can run with.

- **Personalize your pitch.** Your personality can mean money in the bank if you use it to punch up your information. If you use your personality strategically, it can add spice to your story. Just be careful not to overdo it . . . make sure your personality doesn't eclipse or contradict the message you are trying to send.

- **Keep your eye on the ball.** Good press is fantastic, but it's not an end in itself. The end goal is a thriving, successful business. While publicity can certainly help you, it's not going to do the work of building a business for you.

Despite what many a public relations firm will have you believe, the media is not some overly complicated, mythical beast, but a simple and straightforward business. If you think of the media as the middleman between stories and audiences, you'll be able to use the tips in this chapter along with the marketing savvy you picked up in chapter 7 to turn your information into the kind that helps, not hinders, your idea.

10

NOW YOU'RE MOVING

I AM A licensed race car driver. It's true. I have a CAMS license. For those of you unfamiliar with this acronym, it stands for Confederation of Australian Motor Sport. I am looking at my license even as I am writing this. Too bad it's only valid for one race: the 1995 Formula 1 Australian Grand Prix. I was asked to participate in the celebrity Grand Prix, which is held right before the main event and involves Australian celebrities in real racing suits, driving real race cars around the real Formula 1 racetrack. After our race, I got the award for Most Polite Driver and Most Fuel Efficient.

Another way of saying I came in last.

Since I had always considered car racing to be a sport

in name only, the weeklong training course and the race that followed proved to be a rude awakening. Turns out race car driving requires a great deal of strategy and focus as well as nerves of steel. Who knew? In retrospect, it was silly of me to assume that car racing would be scary but not difficult. No form of motion is ever simple.

The type of motion we turn our attention to in this chapter is the kind that's required to keep your business up and running—an entirely different style than what was required to get the business off the ground. This chapter is about what you do once you get "there." In other words, now that you have started a business, got the promotion, received your press coverage, or changed careers, how do you know you are still going in the right direction? How fast should you be going? What signs should you look out for? Should you just floor it or should you be careful? There are so many new and perplexing challenges that arise when you actually get going that it's not unusual to feel a little lost in ways you weren't expecting. But that lost feeling just means that you have shifted gears from start-up to maintenance.

Just like any change, it will take a little while to settle in before you get the hang of this new phase. So strap on your seat belt and come with me for a spin around the racetrack. Let me tell you what I learned about movement on my course.

My Story

I burst into tears in the lower ground area of David Jones. David Jones is one of Australia's most upscale department stores and I had come for a meeting with their cosmetics buyer. My lipsticks had been selling there for over six months, and even though I was locked in an ongoing struggle to get them moved from the lower ground floor to the prestigious first floor, they were doing very well. Remember that Australian "cultural cringe" I told you about, where many homegrown products were considered inferior to the imports? Well, it was alive and kicking in 1993 downtown David Jones. My lipsticks were being sold in the pharmacy section of the store along with the discount brands, even though mine were about four times the price. The buyer couldn't conceive of an Australian lipstick being high-end.

Before heading into the corporate office for my meeting, I stopped to have a look at the lipsticks on display. Before I knew it, tears were welling up and sliding down my cheeks faster than I could wipe them away. On a middle shelf shoved between eyedrops, digestive aids, and cold medicines were a few Poppy lipsticks standing next to a clear acrylic box that could be mistaken for Tupperware. Rattling around inside

that box were some lipstick testers that were probably violating about ten different hygiene codes. And
to make matters even worse, the testers were all open
and smudges of lipsticks were everywhere. It was hor-
rifying to see my brand, my passion, displayed like
this.

I picked up the box and took it with me to the meeting. On the elevator ride up to the buyer's office, my
pain was clearly on display as I fought to curb the wa-
terworks. I got them under control, but my voice was
still shaking when I put the mess of a box down on
the buyer's desk and said, "I have just spent $20,000
advertising this product."

While $20,000 is barely a drop in the bucket in the
grand scheme of cosmetics advertising, to my little
brand, it was a very big deal. It was my first-ever ad,
a full page in *Vogue* and a couple of other magazines.
For the past year I had received so much editorial that
I hadn't needed to advertise, but now things were beginning to level off. I had been covered everywhere,
so there wasn't much more they could write about me.
Also, some competition had appeared on the scene. To
keep the ball rolling, I had decided to take out some
ads.

Not only was there the cost of buying the pages in
the magazine but also the production costs of the ad

itself, which included hiring a photographer, a model, a hairstylist, a makeup artist, and so on. The ad ended up looking great. It was for the seven deadly sins range and communicated luxury and decadence through and through.

To think that we had this eye-catching ad out there and that new customers, or even existing ones, would be coming into David Jones asking where they could find Poppy lipsticks only to be directed to a mess that would put a kid's toy box to shame. We would have been better off attracting fewer customers because the more people who saw the brand looking this awful, the more goodwill would erode. "Goodwill" is the commercial term for reputation. A brand has goodwill in the same way a person has a reputation. Unfortunately, both take longer to build than they do to damage.

In my desperation to keep momentum going with advertising, I hadn't taken into account that pulling people in was not constructive before I did some patching up.

One thing that became apparent in my efforts to further my goals was that movement just for movement's sake is more likely to take you backward instead of forward. I am not suggesting that everything must be perfect before you can go further—if that were the case, no one would ever get beyond the first few steps. There is no need to become a type A personality just to keep something moving. And thank goodness, because I would be doomed. If only you could see my desk right now, you would realize I am hardly the organized type!

The best approach to keeping something moving the way you want is with determination and a commitment not to perfection, but to awareness. While no one can hope to go straight to the top without any taking any detours or wrong turns, we can all attempt to keep our eyes, ears, and minds open as we go forward. When you have achieved something important to you—like starting a business or getting hired for an exciting new job—it is tempting to place the achievement in a protective bubble and see only what you want to see. But doing this actually stunts your ability to capitalize on that achievement and experience real growth. The more willing you are to stay as aware as you were when you were in the process of achieving your initial goal, the higher your chances of achieving many others.

LESSON 49: Watch out for bad omens

As you strive toward new goals there will be signs along the way to point you in the right direction. Some of the most important signs of all revolve around resistance. How much resistance do you feel around any desired course of action?

By resistance I mean, How are things falling into place? What is the consistent response that you are getting from outside people or entities necessary to the plan of action? If, on average, the response is agreeable, with only a few bumps here and there, then things are falling into place well. This is the kind of resistance that is a good sign. Should those bumps turn into a very rugged and rocky terrain, you may want to wait before strapping on your mountain-climbing gear. Stop and ask: Is the universe trying to tell you something? And should you listen?

By no means is this to say that you should give up easily. Can you imagine how many amazing inventions, many of which we take for granted as part of our daily lives, would not exist if people gave up after just a few hiccups? But a constant flow of hiccups, setbacks, and resistance needs to be considered before you decide whether or not to push ahead.

My Story

You may recall that just before I started my lipstick brand, I worked in a lingerie store. It was an upscale boutique in a very chic area, so the men who would

sometimes wander in weren't perverts or creeps, but just fumbling, stammering guys who felt so uncomfortable that they could hardly look you in the eye. Since they were completely unversed in the language of bras and knickers, we were more likely to get a hand gesture than a verbal response when we asked what size his lady friend was.

"Uh, hmmm, oh, I guess she's about this big up top and hmm, uh, ummm say this down below."

After a while, one got the hang of figuring out the sizes from these visual clues. As soon as it was over, the guy would race out of there as fast as he could and that would be the last we would see of him — but not the last we would see of the sale. Nine times out of ten (I kid you not) the recipient of the items would end up back in our store, disheveled gift box in hand, to exchange his choices. "I don't know who my boyfriend thinks I am but these do not fit me," they would say, shaking their heads in exasperation.

It was true; they always got the sizes wrong and always in the same way. The bra was way too big and the panties too small. All these men seemed to think they were going to bed with Pamela Anderson replicas.

Lingerie and fantasy. Lipstick and fantasy. My obsession with glamour led me directly to both. Although lipstick is by far and away my first love, I am also a devotee of fine lingerie—which is why I was continually frustrated by the choices which, back in the mid-1990s, seemed to be limited to three looks: sporty, safe, or slutty.

Where was something chic, something with some flair without being trampy? Something that was not just a slave to men's idea of sexy or women's idea of sensible? Something in between? Sexy in its smartness? Unless you were willing to pay a small fortune for your smalls, the selection in the average department store was pretty dismal.

So in 1996, with a lipstick brand in full swing, I decided to enter the lingerie market and design my own just like I had with the lipsticks. Only this time, it wasn't so easy. I had assumed that it would be much, much easier because I now had a well-known brand name and more than a year's distance between myself and high school. But I was wrong. Whereas most of the people I spoke to about the lipsticks had been somewhat intrigued by the notion of starting a lipstick brand, when it came to my lingerie idea they were just flat.

They—manufacturers, retailers, even people working with me at the time—didn't feel it made any sense for me to go into lingerie as my next big move. They didn't think there was a logical and strong connection. I could manage to assuage some of their concern by explaining the psychological link between lipstick and lingerie and how both revolved around female sexuality. But anything that takes a thesis just to get people to shrug their shoulders and say "maybe" is not a good sign. I did find manufacturers, but then found that most of my efforts were not going into designing, as I had hoped, but into continually reminding them why they were doing this. But despite the constant resistance and lack of enthusiasm that hovered around this project, I kept pushing ahead.

Finally, I got it to market. The product was good but not great. Sure, it had the flair that I felt had been missing in lingerie, but the shapes and fabrics were not quite right. I had all these ideas that were very high-end, yet the only fabric I could afford to use was considerably cheaper and not great quality. One of my styles was called Papillon (French for "butterfly") and featured an embroidered butterfly on each cup of the bra and a little caterpillar on the panties. Nice idea, but with the wrong shape and fabric. It didn't end up how I had envisioned it. Unlike the process I was paying homage to, that of the caterpillar metamorphosing from its cocoon into a butterfly, the whole lingerie venture never really made it. It never did

turn into a butterfly. Sometimes a caterpillar is just a caterpillar, and sometimes you need to accept that Mother Nature knows best.

I realize that looking for signs sounds a little like voodoo or astrology. And I admit, I love reading my horoscope. Even though I don't necessarily believe it—first of all, how could every single Gemini in the world be experiencing the same exciting career prospects on this one day? And do you know how many fascinating and beguiling strangers I should have come across? If all my readings had materialized, I would barely have the time to ponder that puzzling question that has been plaguing me and is about to be solved with the deepening of a relationship close to my heart!

THE RIGHT VERSUS WRONG RESISTANCE

How do you tell whether the kind of resistance you're getting to your next move is the right or wrong sort? I suggest you think of the resistance the same way you would if you were strength training with weights. Before you make any moves, ask yourself:

- **CAN I DO THIS?** How heavy is the load? Does lifting the weight of your next move feel hard but doable, or is something really hurting when you try to lift it? Is there too much financial risk attached? Too many people disagreeing with it? Is it so difficult to put the pieces together that you have to stop everything you are doing? If so, don't drop the weight suddenly, but slowly put it down and figure out what may need adjusting.

- **WILL I GET INJURED?** In other words, are you doing it right? If what you're doing is known to have caused injuries before, figure out why this move has been so difficult for others. Figure out if there is a way to achieve similar results without hurting anything you have already.

- **WHO IS THE BEST PERSON TO HELP ME?** A personal trainer is a luxury that many of us can't afford when we do our workouts, but as far as your work is concerned, you can't afford *not* to find a few people you really trust to give it to you straight. Their opinions may not be what you want to hear, but you will be stronger for having listened, even if you still want to proceed.

Horoscope-speak is great fun, but when it comes to looking for signs that you are on the right track with what you have started, you don't need to go to a fortune-teller. Instead, look at and evaluate the feedback you're getting. Try to understand what is underneath the reactions you receive to your next move. And instead of writing off the resistance of others as groundless, carefully examine the rationale behind their hesitation. Once you've done that, you may still want to continue, or you may not. Check your horoscope if you wish. It could read that something you have been pursuing requires some careful thinking before the right direction will become clear.

Oh yeah . . . and a beguiling stranger is about to enter your circle.

LESSON 50: **Choose or lose**

It is said that success breeds success, but it also breeds something else — choices. We are often required to choose from a plethora of new options while we are still heady from the initial rush of achieving a goal. In this euphoric state, it can be tempting to try everything. Why lose any option? Just do it all.

But doing it all isn't really an option. Well, not a viable one, anyway. To continue your success, you will have to make choices, choices that allow you to see a way forward instead of going round in circles. I learned a lot about this on the racetrack.

Our instructors told us that the most efficient and safest way through the curves on the racecourse was to drive through them in the straightest line possible. This meant that you had to follow an invisible line on the road rather than follow the curve of the road itself. Apparently, the more you follow the curve, the harder it is to keep the car under control whereas going through a straight line enables you to maintain your speed and hold your position. It always felt counterintuitive to me; I thought the safe thing to do would be to go where the road took you. That is, to follow everything that appeared in front of me as thoroughly as I could. As it turns out, this idea is not only dangerous on the racecourse but in the real world as well. Not only does too much going with the flow hinder your ability to take the lead, but it can throw you off track entirely.

Believe me, the regret of making the wrong choice is nothing compared to how you will feel if you end up in a tailspin because you are afraid of saying no, and are trying to do too much.

My Story

I can still see them now. Those little pink message slips showing the name of the person who called, the time, the date, and a brief message, as well as little boxes to tick if they will call back or they are expecting you to call. Even with e-mail, texting, cell phones, and all the other technology around, they are still used in what is becoming a rarer and rarer occurrence—the landline phone call.

In the early days of my business, I relied exclusively on the phone and was always thrilled when the operators of the answering service I had hired handed me a wad of those pink message slips. Article after article was appearing about me and my lipsticks and many of them included the phone number of how to reach me. The girls at the front desk were almost as excited as I was: "Look at all these messages, Poppy. I think your lipstick business is going to be a big success judging by the response."

It sure seemed that way. Most of the messages were either from people requesting an interview or from people who had stores and wanted to sell the lipsticks. Talk about being spoiled for choice. Before I had to convince stores into giving the lipsticks a try and now stores were calling me from all over the country.

Salons, spas, hairdressers, beauty parlors (yes, there were still beauty parlors in those days), jewelry stores, and fashion boutiques . . . everyone wanted these lipsticks. While I may understand what Groucho Marx meant when he said "I don't want to belong to any club that will accept me as a member" as it refers to me personally, when it came to my lipsticks I understood only too well why others loved them as much as I did. And I wanted every store that wanted them to have them. I knew I couldn't double up when it came to location—if one store on a particular street already carried Poppy lipsticks, I wouldn't put them in another store too close by. But other than that, I saw no reason to say no. Why not give them to salons, jewelry stores, and other channels? Isn't that called growth?

Well, yes and no. In one sense, getting new orders and more dollars can be considered growth. But is it constructive growth? In the beginning, the fashion boutiques that carried Poppy had given the brand a great deal of cachet and differentiation. As I started to put the lipsticks into most of the channels that requested them, the image of the brand began to splinter and change. By changing the retail strategy that worked at the beginning, the brand's point of view became less clear, and whatever short-term gains I may have made financially were offset by the weakened marketing strategy. Worse still, I lost credibility from those key boutiques that had been my choices to begin with, and was left with credibility in the stores that had chosen me rather than the other way around.

Avoiding making a choice can be just as dangerous as making the wrong choice. Rely on this avoidance tactic for too long and the decisions may end up being taken out of your hands as others make up their minds for you. And many times, the choices others make for you are not the ones you like but the ones you get stuck with.

While saying no to some options may feel like a sacrifice, whatever loss you feel is often outstripped by gains such as increased clarity, stronger leverage, a firmer grip, and concentrated energy. All of these add up to the biggest advantage there is when it comes to furthering your goals and moving from one success to another: focus. While there is no fast track to ongoing success, focus is certain to keep you in a prime position.

LESSON 51: **Don't follow the competition**

Your ability to focus will prove critical as your success grows and your competitors multiply. Competition—the knowledge that others are out there vying for your spot or worse, coming right at ya—can be very frightening. I remember one point during the celebrity Grand Prix race, when I was zooming down what is known as "the straight," the part of the racecourse where you are able to drive fastest because there are no curves. I was almost at the end of the straight, when I looked in my rearview mirror to see about seven cars racing toward me at extremely high speeds. It's not what you think . . . I wasn't ahead. On the contrary, because I was so much slower than many of the other drivers, I was being lapped. *Eek!*

Luckily, our instructors had prepared us for just this scenario: "The worst thing the car being lapped can do is try to move over and make room for the others to pass. Stick to your line, just keep driving as if they aren't there, and let them get around you. We have seen so many accidents happen when a driver panics and tries to change lanes."

While the advice made perfect sense to me, when you are in the moment, with a cluster of speeding cars coming up behind you, it is easier to say than do. I just breathed and tried to remember what I had been told. "Stick to your line, stick to your line. It is their problem to get around you." It worked. No lipstick entrepreneurs were harmed in the making of this anecdote. I have also used the same strategy when it comes to dealing with competition in the nonracing world. Take a deep breath and stick to your line.

When you see someone or something breathing down your neck, your natural reflex is to act immediately and go on the defense. Yet, often, your best move is to keep going the way you are going. As they say in sports, the best defense is a good offense. All that means is doing exactly what you've been doing before you became aware of the competition. After all, you were already going in a particular direction for a reason. Remember your reasons and try not to let the competition spook you into no longer believing them.

My Story

Sassy. That was the name of the first competition that sprung up after my lipsticks became a runaway success. I was terrified. When I heard that someone else was bringing out a small line of lipsticks to be sold in fashion boutiques, I felt like I had been punched in the stomach. Usually when I had that feeling it was from finding out that a guy I liked had his eye on someone else. That horrible sinking feeling when you physically buckle under the weight of what you just heard. Yuck. There is nothing worse.

Never having faced down any competition in business before (but plenty in my love life!), I became very worried about Sassy. I had no idea what would happen if a similar product was introduced into my stores. Also, I was a still a teenager and had yet to learn about the cool, professional approach. Instead, I took the morbid approach.

"What if this ends my business?" I asked my close friends and family, "What if no one buys Poppy lipsticks anymore?"

For all the anxiety it caused me, Sassy may as well have been the end. If I wasn't running out to buy every magazine the moment it hit the stands just to check if there was anything about this upcoming line, I was pestering my friends to patrol various fashionable neighborhoods. I stopped making any independent decisions. "Let's just see what the effects of Sassy will be before we do that" became my answer to everything.

Everyone told me I was worrying too much, but these words had about as much effect on me as they would on Woody Allen waiting for the results of a biopsy. Whatever the diagnosis, I was convinced it would be terminal. I know it must seem odd to you that I was making all this fuss over this brand; didn't I have enormous competition already? Didn't the names Estée Lauder, Revlon, and Clinique ring any bells for me? Yes, but they didn't scare me. Their products, their marketing, everything about them was so different that it was because of and not despite them that I decided to start my own business.

What scared me about Sassy was that it was going to be so close to the "indie" mood of my brand. Living all the way over in Australia before the Internet, I had no idea that I was not alone and that other cosmetics brands had hatched that were also rebelling against the traditional makeup houses. Brands such as MAC, Bobbi Brown, and Stila. All of us came about in different ways but for a lot of the same reasons, and even though I was on the other side of the Pacific Ocean and barely out of high school, I somehow had caught the same vibe. Now that someone on my own turf was onto the vibe, I was panicking.

In the end, the biggest impact Sassy ever had on my brand was the impact it had on me. Being first to market gave me a head start that Sassy was never able to catch up to. The loss was not in customers, but in time and energy wasted on worrying about what was around me rather than on what lay ahead.

Just as imitation is the sincerest form of flattery, competition is the sincerest indication that you are doing something right. No one competes for something unless they see a future in it. When you're faced with rivals, it's important to remember that focusing on the competition takes just as much energy as keeping the focus on yourself and furthering your goals. Except no one has ever built a business by stressing about the competition. Having wasted way too much energy on worrying, I'd advise you to put your own efforts to constructive use. Instead of racking your brain for ways to defeat your opponents, keep your mind on how to grow your business and stick to your line.

LESSON 52: **Some rules aren't meant to be broken**

Just because I and all my indie buddies overseas may have had success rebelling against a conventional approach to marketing doesn't mean that every rule can be broken with impunity. Although we've known that rebellion can be an image booster ever since the days of James Dean, there are some areas where tried and trusted principles are tried and trusted because they work. The trick is to determine in which areas to improvise and in which to stick to the script.

A unique or unconventional approach can work wonders when you're dealing with matters that are not easily measured—subjective matters, such as marketing. In many cases, the reason there are no reliable means of measurement is that it has not been possible to come up with any, so there's really no choice but to experiment and be creative. On the flip side, experience has taught me that in those areas that can be measured, rules usually apply for a good reason. Take the example of money. One dollar represents 100 cents—this is a rule and convention that is well-defined, completely entrenched, and thoroughly accepted. You could decide that from now on one dollar of yours will represent 150 cents, but what chances do you think you stand of convincing the rest of the world to do the same? And what is your reasoning for wanting to challenge it anyway? Is there something that is not working with the existing measurement? Can you imagine how much good effort you would expend trying to change this when you could be concentrating on putting those efforts elsewhere?

Any pursuit will have its objective arena filled with formulas, procedures, measurements, conventions, and yes, rules. And while this doesn't mean that you always need to stick to them, you would be wise to acknowledge and understand them before you decide whether or not to dismiss them.

My Story

The business had hit a number of plateaus in Australia that were holding us up both domestically and internationally. Retailers all over the world were interested in taking the line (even someone in Siberia!), but while I had managed to get a great lipstick out of a little manufacturing plant, when I tried to get other products from the same facility, the quality just wasn't right for my audience. And since no other Australian cosmetics brands were selling in stores like Barneys, for example, the pressure was really on to find ways to release new products that could compete in upscale environments.

While Australia has a great deal of opportunity, it is not at the forefront of cosmetics innovation compared to, say, the United States. So I brought in a top New York City executive search firm to identify renowned cosmetics chemists and approach them on behalf of my dynamic independent brand (a "renovator's delight" as they say in the real estate world). After narrowing down the respondents, one guy seemed like the best fit. Color products were his forte and he had been very involved in the development of a hugely successful and innovative lipstick. We needed someone like him.

It took a great deal of time, effort, and logistics for me to find someone like that who was willing to move to Australia. It also took quite a good deal of money to bring him over—money that we did not yet have. Although we were profitable, we needed more money to grow and expand our products and markets. But the cost associated with both of these areas is front-loaded, meaning that you have to spend money before you make it. It's a textbook-style growing pain with textbook-style answers. So many businesses have confronted and dealt with these exact same problems that we now have formulas and conventions that are proven methods to grow a business.

As any textbook from economics to business to pure physics will tell you, to safely make the leap from one platform to the next, you have to solidify your existing platform before developing any maneuvers in the air. No matter how good your gymnastics, without something solid to jump off of and land on, you are bound to get hurt—which is exactly what happened when I ignored conventional thinking and, rather than investing my time, effort, and resources into securing funding first and a new chemist to engineer new products second, I did it the other way around.

I went and got the talent first and then shifted my attention to the funding, or should I say finding the solid wooden planks of the next platform. I thought it would make it easier for us to get investment if we could show that we were two steps ahead by having a top-level chemist on board who was ready and waiting to develop new products. Ready and waiting. Therein lay the flaw in my logic. Until I had further investment to set him up in a lab, there was nothing for him to do but sit around chewing up dollars with his salary.

My aerial acrobatics had real impact on the financials of the business and started a bleeding that was now in desperate need of money to stop. And desperate is not how you want to be when you are looking for investors. This wouldn't have been the case if I had

looked for investors first and a chemist second. The cart does not pull the horse.

Like I said, some rules aren't meant to be broken. Not everything requires an unconventional approach, and neither does being conventional in certain areas mean that you can't be innovative in others. It is not a zero-sum game. One does not cancel out the other. What you really need is a bit of both—innovation along with rule observation. The dot-com mania of the late nineties confirmed this for me. I was shocked that all these people (kids in many cases) were finding money so easily with nothing solid to show. Having been put through the wringer trying to find financing myself, even with a track record, I began to question my hard-won understanding of the rules concerning stable business practice. But as it turned out, the new economy was not all that different from the old. Even in this virtual world full of mavericks, visionaries, rule breakers, and pioneers, many time-tested rules and conventions still applied.

LESSON 53: The long and the short of it

Any given action can hold two meanings: the meaning it has for now and the meaning it may have for later. When it comes to furthering your goals, you have to keep one eye on the here and now and the other on more far-off points, making sure to assess and weigh both the short- and long-term consequences of your actions.

This advice is hard to follow when you have to sacrifice short-term comfort for a longer-term payoff. While most of us find this extremely difficult, it is an extremely worthwhile skill to foster. As the saying goes, better the pain of discipline today than the pain of regret tomorrow.

Fortunately, you don't need to sacrifice immediate satisfaction all the time, since too much emphasis on the long term with no regard to the here and now can be just as dangerous as the opposite. The ability to alternate between what is good for the time being and what is good for the future makes the difference between fleeting and sustainable success. Too many shortsighted solutions too close together tend to weaken your business and pose a real risk to your future.

My Story

This is not so much my story as it is Estée Lauder's, the legendary cosmetics entrepreneur and inventor of the famous "gift with purchase" promotion. Now widely practiced across many industries, the concept of giving something away for free with a purchase was new to customers back when Mrs. Lauder first began enticing them to splurge and then rewarding them with a gift. And while reward was her original intention, she also knew that it would be a win-win proposition: customer gets something for free and feels special. Customer begins to associate good feeling with Estée Lauder. Customer tries free product sample. If customer likes product, purchases a full-size one next time. Customer gets new gift and same cycle begins again.

Estée Lauder tapped into the psychology of getting something for free. She understood that it is not so much about the thing itself as it is about the feeling that goes along with getting something for nothing. Even the rich and famous are mesmerized by freebies. In fact, not so long ago I was at the Chanel makeup counter at Bergdorf Goodman, one of the most expensive stores in the world, when I saw a customer rustling around inside her little shopping bag with all the decorum of your average squirrel. "Didn't I get anything free with that?" she asked. "I thought I would get some samples."

Up until that point I had been intently examining the difference between two lipstick shades but was now far more interested in the woman next to me. I took her in from head to toe—all $80,000 of her. That was my eyeball estimate of the value of what I could see on her person, let alone what was inside her $9,000

Birkin bag. I am not exaggerating, perhaps even underestimating as I am not as good at appraising jewelry and plastic surgery procedures as I am at clothing and accessories. And here she was, devastated because she didn't get her free samples! More than retail therapy was needed here.

Somewhere along the line the whole GWP (gift with purchase) concept went completely insane. And as is often the case, underneath insane behavior lies a pattern of abuse. The concept began to get abused and used as a short-term fix. Not by the customer (although as my story above demonstrates, the customer may abuse it too) but by the brands. The immediate spike it produced in sales was too tempting to resist and the GWP soon became a Band-Aid solution for lagging sales.

The more one brand did it, the more another had to follow suit in order to compete both for the customer's and the retailer's attention. Every year a brand has to make at least the numbers from last year and preferably demonstrate growth. So if you had a very successful GWP one year, you have to match it the next; otherwise, your numbers look bad to the store. And to make it successful once everyone started doing it, the gift offering had to get more and more tempting. Suddenly, a free perfume and cream sample no longer seemed quite as attractive.

It's gotten so that I am now willing to pay extra to *not* get any free junk. This is one of the reasons why trendy brands such as MAC don't do GWPs. Whereas the original intention was to give both the brand and the customer cachet, the GWP now does neither. But it is too late. Those in the cosmetics and retail industry are now stuck in a problem of their own making. Brands now feel obligated to give out freebies — and rather than feeling special when they get something, customers are more likely to feel slighted when they don't.

You can't achieve long-term goals with short-term solutions. That's why it's so crucial you look out for not only what's right in front of you, but what lies ahead. Of course, only hindsight is 20/20 and you can never know exactly what's coming up around the bend, but if you make sure to keep your short-term solutions in line with your long-term goals, your success will prove far longer-lasting and more sustainable.

Conclusion

I remember one particular moment back in 1996 like it was yesterday. I was driving on a Los Angeles highway to meet with the buyers for a huge chain of U.S. department stores. On the passenger seat were maps, scribbled directions from the concierge at my hotel, empty water bottles, my handbag, and a box of lipstick samples. The buyers knew my line was in Barneys and now they wanted it too. They had contacted me all the way over in Australia to set up a meeting. This was a big fish and the type of account that can be the difference between having a small business and a big one. Everyone back in the office was very excited about this—except me. I knew we weren't ready for something of this size despite the fact that I wished we were.

I had been in business for about four years now and had enough history to know that it was all too easy to mess up something this big out of impatience. It would have been amazing to come home from this trip with huge orders for, say, forty of their one hundred or so stores. The zeros on that check would have been exhilarating. But then what? How would we really be able to be successful in their stores once the lipsticks were on their counters? We would need salespeople, infrastructure, monitoring, training . . . all these aspects that we didn't have set up in the United States and couldn't afford just yet. So here I was, driving toward the head offices of a powerful retailer only to let them down. To say no and admit I wasn't ready.

I was thinking about how much I would have loved

to be in a different position, when suddenly, out there on that L.A. highway, I realized that the position I was in was pretty fantastic already. I was a world away from home, doing my own thing, and living my dream because of everything I had done to date. The good, the bad, and the indifferent . . . all of it had allowed me to have this moment of clarity which, in turn, would no doubt contribute to the opportunities that still lay ahead.

Past, present, future. In times of careful consideration you can see and appreciate the effect of all three. It's no different in idea actualization. To stay aware and focused at all times you have to keep an eye on what's going on around you now, what you and others have learned in the past, and what may await you in the future. No one is saying it's easy, least of all me, but you can do it if you:

- **Read the signs.** Resistance is your clearest and most obvious sign of trouble ahead. If you're finding that too many obstacles are popping up between you and your goals, don't just barrel ahead but ask yourself if it may be time to reconsider.

- **Act decisively.** At times of success, entrepreneurs are often tempted to spread themselves too thin. When this happens, remind yourself that you can't possibly follow up on every lead and still stay focused.

Then start practicing saying one very important word: *no*.

- **Stick to your line.** Once the world gets a whiff of your success, there is bound to be competition. But don't let rivals deter you from pursuing your goals. Just remember that the best defense is a good offense. Stay focused on growing your business.

- **Play by the time-tested rules.** Creativity and innovation have their limits. In certain areas, you'll do well to consider and follow conventional wisdom. Many of the established rules have come from the trials and errors of others in the past, and we can benefit from their experience by not dismissing these rules too quickly.

- **Look both ways before you act.** Lengthen the life span of your success by staying mindful of the long- and short-term consequences of your decisions. Sometimes, you have to sacrifice immediate gratification for the future good of your business.

Arriving somewhere is just the beginning of going on to somewhere else. Life is in constant motion and so are our dreams, goals, desires, ambitions, and challenges. What may have gotten you to one position could be different from what is required for the road ahead. To keep the success you have earned to date and position yourself for more to come, you have to keep your eyes open and be prepared to shift gears. If you learn from what's come before, pay attention to what's around you, and never stop planning for what could be. You're bound to find the right gear and the right direction no matter where you find yourself. True success has no finish line.

11

TO ERR IS HUMAN

EVERYONE POOPS.

This is the title of a wildly popular children's book about, you guessed it, poop. When I first heard about this book, I couldn't really understand why kids would be so attracted to the subject. I didn't think much of it again until writing this chapter about mistakes, and the title just popped into my head. Mistakes get treated like poop. We know they happen. We know they aren't pleasant. But just like poop, mistakes are a regular part of life. While kids are fascinated by poop and all the bodily noises, odors, fluids, and machinations that go hand in hand with being human, adults are not. Somewhere along the line, the switch happens. Instead of celebrating being human, we start seeing it as something to contain and even deny.

In work, relationships, lifestyle, and many other areas, we often set standards for ourselves that border on the superheroic. Any time we refuse to accept our mistakes we are refusing to allow ourselves a basic right — the right not to be perfect, the right not to even expect it. Believe it or not, you can expect your best, and most successful people do, yet still allow for mistakes.

Mistakes are going to happen whether you like it or not, so prepare for them by acknowledging that not even the worst mistake is all bad. On the contrary, mistakes can:

- Increase your esteem through the new knowledge and understanding that comes from them
- Enhance your willingness to experience new things as you become less fearful of them
- Improve your serenity by showing you that life goes on even after them

But to get all these goodies from mistakes will require that you develop some coping strategies. None of us are born with the ability to deal with our mistakes gracefully. Fortunately, coping skills are like muscles: the more you use them the stronger they become.

You can start developing these skills by doing what I

do—realizing that very few mistakes are as bad as they feel. By separating the discomfort of making a mistake from the actual mistake itself, you can learn to accept that making mistakes doesn't make you bad or stupid . . . it just makes you human.

My Story

How fitting that I should be writing about mistakes in chapter 11 since the lowest point of my career to date was when my business went into the Australian equivalent of Chapter 11. Chapter 11 of the U.S. Bankruptcy Code allows a troubled business legal protection from creditors as it reorganizes its debts, sells any assets, and distributes the proceeds to a hierarchy of entities who are owed money. In other words, Chapter 11 is when the $#%@ hits the fan and you have no other option left because the business is not in good enough shape to get further investment or bank loans or any other constructive financing.

My business troubles were attributable entirely to a pattern of mistakes that can be traced back to long before the actual consequence. While its "Chapter 11" may have signified the actual collapse, the company had been ailing for quite some time from a series of misguided decisions and an even worse business partnership.

One of the two major mistakes that led me into this misguided partnership was funding the talent before the business (remember that very expensive chemist?). The other was mismanaging my own skills by looking for investment funding myself instead of hiring someone with proper expertise to do this for me. These two screw-ups led to the worst screw-up of all — entering a business partnership situation where the fit was all wrong. None of us deliberately set out to make it as bad and untenable as it became, but no one could undo the chain of events that earlier mistakes set into motion.

Fortunately, wherever you have mistakes, you also have the opportunity for recovery. Even if a business cannot recover from the mistakes of the humans who run it, the humans can. I did. And even my business did to some extent. After we went into the equivalent of Chapter 11, the company was sold to a new owner (a little like a fire sale) and the Poppy brand went on for another four years. It was, however, only a shadow of its former self.

Now that some years have passed, I can honestly say that the opposite is true of me. As much as I have hurt, suffered, and grieved through everything that went on, I am much stronger as a result of living and learning through these mistakes.

As humans, we have the capacity for many emotions, each with its own corresponding cycles and phases. Since mistakes cause us grief (often much more than necessary), let's explore the five psychological phases of grief—denial, anger, bargaining, depression, and acceptance—as they relate to making mistakes. This should help us not only move past our mistakes, but surpass them and emerge that much stronger out the other side.

LESSON 54: Stop the *denial*

The most immediate of reactions to bad news is denial. As in, "Oh no! This can't be happening. How can I stop it from being true? How can I get out of it, avoid it, get rid of it?" As it dawns on us that we may have made a mistake, our first response may be to bury it. Cover it up. After all, if you make a mistake in a forest but no one is there to see it, did it really happen?

The answer, of course, is yes, it did! Burying mistakes has a tendency of just making matters worse. Whether your mistake was honest or deceptive, big or small, the cover-up often serves only to aggravate an already sour situation.

Of all the destructive reactions you can have to a mistake, denial is one of the worst. It robs you of the ability to get past the mistake and limits you to desperate avoidance tactics. The antidote to denial is honesty. If you want to deal with your mistake effectively, you have to tell yourself the truth both about what went wrong and how you feel about the results. Sure, this may be uncomfortable, but the more discomfort you feel around the mistake, the more you need to explore why and understand what is behind it in order to move ahead.

My Story

Recently I was waiting in line at a store to pay for something. Instead of the usual "next customer" drill, the person at the open register said "I can take care of you." What a lovely thought. It is so nice to be taken care of. It feels so good to trust that someone knows what they are doing and is taking care of stuff. Elvis loved the concept so much he emblazoned TCB everywhere. It stood for Taking Care of Business.

So many times when I had this person or that doing various roles, I assumed that they were TCB—taking care of business—which is a fine premise to have until proven otherwise. But once it becomes clear that they aren't doing a good, or even sane, job and that change is not possible, denial of that can be very seductive. It is a bummer, to say the least, to acknowledge that someone is not in fact TCB and may in actually BDB—Be Destroying Business. I once went so far into denial of this with someone I wanted to believe in that things had to get pretty bad before I was willing to confront the denial and do the necessary damage control. People were negatively affected as a result of this denial, not least of all me. My denial may have started out as a protective response but the consequences of it were anything but. To this day I am haunted by what happened. I even dream about it all of the time, which shows that the subconscious is wise and a force to be reckoned with. I denied it and found it to be literally at my peril. I shudder to think what could have happened had I and this other person stayed in that dangerous state any longer.

When it comes to mistakes, you're better off doing what you can to fix them today rather than putting the unpleasantness off until tomorrow. That dark cloud that hovers over you when you know you have to deal with a mistake is often far scarier than the actual act of confronting your mistake head-on. And that's exactly what denial feels like—a black cloud that puts a damper on everything, denying us not only the grief of the problem, but the pleasure of a solution.

LESSON 55: Use anger with caution

"I'm mad as hell and I'm not going to take it anymore!"

These are the words made famous by Howard Beale,

the fictional newsroom anchor in the 1976 movie *Network*. The film revolves around a network news anchor who is fired due to low ratings after years of heading the news. But instead of bowing out gracefully, he decides to expose the hypocrisy and cynicism of some of the modern media by ranting on live television about the exploitation of the viewers. In doing so he becomes an icon and a somewhat deranged guru—and serves as a great example of how sometimes anger can be profitable and worthwhile.

Anger can mobilize and inspire. It can highlight injustice and it can help right wrongs. It is an important emotion in a range of human responses. When used to the exclusion of all other responses, however, any profit that may result from anger is usually offset by the costs. Energy, growth, and learning are all hampered by too much anger. When used without moderation, anger cheats you out of understanding both your own behavior and the behavior of others. Just like its close cousin, denial, it can lock you into the most static of positions and rob you of development.

My Story

My second range of seven lipsticks came out one year after the first seven. Having named the first batch after positive words, I went over to the dark side to do a range of shades named after the seven deadly sins.

When it came to the sin of anger, I chose to match it with a strong, vibrant red.

After looking up different technical and historical aspects of red, I found that there's a reason we say we see red when we're angry. Turns out that "the physical effect of red is said to be such that exposure to quantities of the color quickens the heart rate, prompts the release of adrenaline into the bloodstream, and engenders a sense of warmth." All that just from looking at it!

While angry people may get hot around the collar, they don't exactly engender a "sense of warmth." Angry people are frightening; it is very hard to feel warm and fuzzy about someone who is yelling. I have worked closely with two very angry people. One would explode almost like a firebomb, while the other one was the opposite and would go ice cold with rage. They were both equally terrifying. And never more so than when they had to deal with a mistake they had made. Their immediate response was to get angry at the messenger — usually me.

In my rush to calm them down, I would start making my own mistakes by doing or saying whatever I could to appease. Instead of holding firm to what I believed, I would cave and then enter my own anger cycle. Mine is more of the "get angry at yourself" variety. Although this may make me a little more popular than my "get angry at others" colleagues, it is no less damaging. First, I would get mad at myself for capitulating, then for not having the guts to do anything more about it. That anger would eventually subside, only to turn into resentment of the other person. In the end, since none of us dealt responsibly with our anger, all three of us suffered because of it.

My relationship with both of these people and their effect on me and the business could have been so much more productive, but the problem is that anger is truly blinding. Apparently it's the same with the color red. When I looked it up, I also found that it's "a bossy color, it grabs the attention and overrules all the surrounding colors." What a pity to sacrifice all the other feelings for the sake of just one bossy emotion.

Left unchecked, anger can steamroll right over emotions such as empathy, practicality, rationality, and humility—all very important comrades in getting past a mistake and becoming the better for it. So the key with anger is not to cut it out entirely but instead to monitor it. Make sure you're in control of your anger, and not the other way around. Give it just enough leeway to motivate you to get the job done, then allow other, more constructive emotions to take over.

ANGER MANAGEMENT

While some people think of anger as a sin, it really isn't—
not unless it's indulged to excess. To make sure your anger
is working for you and not against you, don't waste your
time punching at walls and pillows. Instead, try the following
techniques to get a handle on your emotions:

- Ask yourself, Did I or this person do this on purpose
  or was it simply carelessness? Sometimes, just the act
  of acknowledging that the anger-inducing incident
  wasn't done intentionally or to hurt you makes the
  anger dissipate.

- Think about what staying angry is going to accomplish.
  Imagine how the situation will play out if you stay angry versus what will happen if a cooler head prevails.

- Ask yourself if and why you're holding on to the anger.
  Then envision yourself letting it go.

- Hit the gym. Go jogging. Take a kickboxing class. Take
  yourself out of the anger-inducing situation and exert
  some energy.

- Practice yoga and meditation to learn relaxation and
  calming techniques. I love Bikram yoga and I find it
  helps me keep a level head during stressful moments
  in the day. Meditation is known to do the same.

- Imagine yourself years from now. Think back to mistakes you and other people have made. They passed eventually. This will too, and all the sooner if you don't let anger stand in the way of dealing constructively with the problem.

- Think about yourself as a little kid or any other little kid you know. Would you be saying the angry things in your head to that kid? No. You would try instead to calm the situation down, instead of riling things up.

LESSON 56: Bargaining isn't the answer

Back when I lived in Australia, we used to go on holiday to Bali regularly because it was just a short flight away. But no matter how many times I'd visit, I could never get comfortable with the constant solicitation from the local traders to buy everything from sarongs to fake Rolexes to "Bo Derek circa 1979" hairdos. I would always start out with the best intentions, trying to answer each approach with a polite "No, thank you." But after just a few hours, I looked like Britney Spears running from the paparazzi. The only time that I would seek out these traders was when I needed transportation. At times, when haggling with the drivers, I have gotten hung up on the difference between say 15,000 and 16,000 Indonesian rupiah, only to realize that the 1,000 rupiah in question is approximately ten cents!

I know it seems ridiculous, but that's bargaining for you. It's not always rational, particularly not as it appears in the third of the five stages of grief, when it usually manifests itself as desperate promises to give more to charity, be nicer to your mom, or eat healthy for the rest of your life if only something works out in your favor. For me, bargaining looks a bit more like debating. The topic of this debate is always the same: How bad was the mistake I made?

My brain can split into two opposing teams to carry on the following heated debate:

It Wasn't So Bad. No One Will Notice.
Stay Quiet and It Will Go Away.

versus

Significant Error. May Cause Problems Down the Line.
Better Address It Immediately.

While both sides have persuasive arguments, I have to admit that I am not sure you can make mistakes disappear entirely. Mistakes don't lie dormant forever, but return to impact our lives once again at some later date. The good news is that the more aware you are of the likelihood of a mistake coming back to haunt you, the more motivated you are to deal with it as it arises.

My Story

My favorite part of giving speeches is, without a doubt, the Q and A after the main presentation. If I could, I would speak for five minutes maximum and have the rest be question and answer. It is the spontaneity that makes this part so much more satisfying than the speech itself. Sometimes, even I am surprised by my own answers!

Not so long ago I gave a speech to the American National Association of Women Business Owners. I had finished my scribbled prepared piece and was fielding questions when someone asked:

"Could you name any business books that have been valuable in teaching you about business?"

I don't think I had ever been asked this before. Usually I was asked to name role models, not books. I thought about it for a second and then said something strange but utterly heartfelt.

"*Anna Karenina.*"

The audience giggled thinking I was joking. Tolstoy is not generally associated with a genre that gave us such titles as *The 7 Habits of Highly Effective People.*

"Hear me out," I said, while giggling myself. *"Anna Karenina* and many of the other classics have taught me a lot about business."

And I went on to explain that at the heart of these tales are often issues of morality and choice. None of the characters ever seem to truly escape their own actions and decisions. My experience in business has only confirmed what these books say, that the impact of mistakes is cumulative and that nothing really evaporates into the ether. All our actions are like the single stitches in a tapestry that ultimately create the whole picture.

Many Shakespeare, Tolstoy, and Dickens characters could have avoided their sticky ends had they accepted that there would be consequences for their actions, their mistakes. Luckily, it is not too late for us. Our actions today can always make for a better tomorrow.

So forget trying to bargain down the impact of your mistake and the accompanying debate over whether or not you should even bother to rectify the situation. Instead, think of what a great bargain it is to address something in the present and have the benefits continue well into the future. Just as mistakes are cumulative, so are the benefits that come with dealing with them. The strength and understanding you gain from acknowledging and rectifying a mistake accumulates and, before you know it, you have both the wisdom to avoid making unnecessary errors and the competence to deal with them should they arise.

LESSON 57: How to bounce back from depression

Making peace with my hair has been one of the best things about getting older. A cause of great angst in my teens and a power struggle in my twenties, my hair is a frustrating mix of curls in all the wrong places and frizz in the rest. To make matters worse, my hairstyles over the years combine to form something of a hall of shame. First there was that disastrous attempt at a bob with shaved back and sides, and . . . wait for it . . . a tail. Then there was that blond lightening spray that gave me bright orange highlights. There was also a very nasty incident with a wash-in red hair dye that refused to wash out. And I'll never forget the bright idea to permanently straighten my hair, nor the disastrous consequences of having to watch most of it break off. Finally, there was the decade of professional blow-outs and their side effect—a pathological fear of rain.

Then, I hit my thirties and faced New York City summers by deciding it was time to surrender to my curls. Now, I actually like them. Well, most days.

There is a difference between surrendering and giving up. Surrendering can be the first step toward a solution. Giving up, on the other hand, isn't a solution but a reaction, a reaction to depression. When it comes to making mistakes it is easy to feel depressed and mired in the problem. But while problems are depressing, solutions are sufficiently compelling to lift you right out of your blues.

Pantene realized the important psychological distinction between focusing on the problem versus the solution. In recent years, the hair-care giant made a distinct change in how it spoke to its consumer and watched its sales go from enormous to ginormous in the process. Instead of categorizing its products according to the hair type you *have*, it began to categorize its products around the hair type you *want*. Now when you peruse their products, you no longer have to think about your hair in such depressing terms as "dry," "brittle," "oily," or even the boring old notion of "normal." Instead, you're faced with decidedly more attractive options like "smooth and sleek," "relaxed and natural," and "sheer volume." By selling the solution instead of the problem, Pantene has quickly become the bestselling shampoo on the planet.

You can use the same logic to tackle your mistakes. If you focus on working out solutions instead of worrying about the problem, you can turn something that would have been negative into a positive.

My Story

How do you get a whole country to vote down a referendum that most of its people want? If it sounds a bit like a riddle, it was. I'm referring to the debate I mentioned in a previous chapter about whether or not Australia should become a republic, which was voted on in a 1999 referendum. I will spare you the long and boring explanation of the Australian constitution except to remind you that as it stands, Australia is still technically under British rule despite having operated as an independent nation for decades.

Prior to that 1999 referendum, polls showed that a majority of Australians felt Australia should become a republic and have its own head of state (instead of the queen of England). What happened between the polls and the vote on the referendum? The Constitutional Convention, that's what. A convention that I attended as a delegate during the scorching summer of 1998.

For two weeks, approximately 150 people suspended normal life to sit in our old Parliament House and debate whether Australia should make this change. Half of the delegates were appointed by the Australian government and half were elected by the Australian people. I was there as a result of the latter. Some of us supported the change and some were against it. But that wasn't the only difference among us. There was a huge variation as to what we all did for a living and what our backgrounds were. There were ministers of the church, retired politicians, TV talk show hosts, sports commentators, trucking magnates, lawyers, writers, and, yes, even a lipstick queen. Basically anyone who had been hotheaded and outspoken enough to have publicly debated the issue prior to this talk fest.

While these two weeks were certainly fascinating as an anthropological experiment, they were not so effective for those of us who wanted the change. Why? Simple. We were unable to effectively articulate a solution. Both sides appeared to be in a constant dialogue about problems. Problems between people, problems between views, problems around how to make the change and what changes to make and when to make the change. Problems of etiquette, decorum, credibility. You name it and there was a problem. No wonder this convention did not inspire a great deal of confidence in the viewing public. Since no one could articulate a clear and effective alternative, we wound up with the status quo.

Had the overall tone of those two weeks been one of solution rather than problem, the whole thing could have ended very differently. Since I have been living overseas, I have found it very hard to explain why Australia voted down its own independence, which from afar can seem like a strange thing to do. The best way I can explain it to those unfamiliar with the politics, media, and psyche of Australia is to say that only confidence can move something forward, and, right or wrong, we were unable to win the confidence of the people.

You can't find confidence in the problems but you can find it in the solutions. Everyone is attracted to solutions. People seek them out through advice, scholars look for them in books, companies pay for them through consultants . . . solutions are valuable commodities. So start focusing on the solutions and see how fast you go from feeling bad about your mistake to feeling good about trying to fix it.

LESSON 58: Acceptance is the key

This is it. The final of the five established phases of grief: acceptance. After acceptance comes all the good stuff . . . growth, understanding, knowledge, and even fun. The ability to accept your own mistakes means you are well and truly on your way to success. And the more you can accept yourself and accept the fact that you, I, and everyone else makes mistakes, the more success you have to look forward to.

The plain truth of it is that there can be no success without failure. The two go hand in hand for absolutely everyone from Bill Gates to your local deli owner. Take it from someone who has had her mistakes splashed all over the papers: Underneath all the worry about what others may think of us if we make a mistake lies a far more pressing issue—what will we think of ourselves?

Maintaining our own good opinion of ourselves is the true challenge of making mistakes. I am continually surprised by the ease with which many others will accept my mistakes compared to how difficult it is for me to do the same. But allowing for mistakes, and even going so far as to embrace them as a necessary and inevitable part of the learning process, is the key to self-acceptance.

My Story

My lipstick brand started on a tram and ended on one twelve years later. Back when I had neither a car nor a driver's license, trams had served as my main mode of transportation to and from appointments. In fact, I dreamed up the vast majority of my lipstick plans while staring out tram windows. So on the day that my company was officially going to end, I decided to pay tribute to those early days by riding the tram into the city to sign the legal documents that would close my brand and begin my life in New York.

It was the very definition of a sentimental journey—particularly the tram ride home. The documents were signed. The brand as I knew it was now over, my entire adult life as I had known it was over, and I was about to leave my home country for a whole new world to start from the beginning again. So there I was on the tram with over a decade of memories behind me. What a ride it had been!

Had I ever imagined that I would make and lose millions of dollars, become a national hero and then a national controversy, travel all over the world, go to political conventions, win awards, meet both amazing and diabolical people, and everything in between? When I was on the tram all those years ago, did I ever think I would have so many triumphs and make so many mistakes? Did I ever imagine that this day would come to bring an era of my life to a close? And if I did imagine it, then how did I imagine it? I am sure it wouldn't have been like this: back on a tram with nothing to show for all of the above.

When all was said and done, the only tangible thing I left those law offices with was the tram ticket I was holding in my hand. I had long ago lost my place in the millionaire club and now I had no financial security. I was no longer the golden child of Australia. I was not fabulous, or a straightforward success, or a member of any elite. My mistakes along the way had prevented all of these outcomes. Instead, I was just a girl on a tram, just as I'd been the day I started.

Only this time, I had behind me experiences I could never have dreamed of. Good and bad experiences that combined to make me one of the luckiest girls in the world despite the loss of fame and fortune. I mean it. It sounds corny, but despite losing the material wealth, I felt rich in ways I would not have understood all those years ago.

It gets cornier. I actually began to cry on that tram ride. Tears rolled down my cheeks as I stared at that tram ticket and everything it represented. There were tears of sadness, tears of shock, joy, wisdom, trauma, and also laughter. Here I was with a $1.70 tram ticket that was more valuable to me than a Harvard business degree. I had learned so much in those twelve years — far too much to think of that ticket as an ending.

I knew that the ticket I was holding was also a ticket for future journeys. And I have kept it all these years. It sits in a frame on my desk at home and has sat near me the entire time I have been writing this book. That ticket is one of the most valuable possessions I own. I can tell you I wouldn't sell it for a million dollars. That ticket is my ticket to life. As long as I have it, it serves to remind me that success and failure are byproducts of having dreams — and dreams are the most important thing I can ever own.

The more you live life, the more chances you have to make mistakes, but—and here is my main point—it goes both ways: The more chances you have for success as well. Remember, we are not defined by our mistakes or by our success, but by our experiences of both. The sooner you accept your mistakes as a normal, healthy, and vital part of who you are rather than the sum of who you are, the better you will be at getting over them, learning from them, and growing stronger as a result.

Conclusion

No two ways about it, mistakes cause grief. It is tempting to imagine that life would be much better without any failures or errors, but would it really?

I went through so much grief with my business that I never thought I would start another one again. People always said to me, "Oh you're an entrepreneur through and through. You will start your own thing again." But I always thought, No way, no how. I will never go through that grief again. I made my mistakes, end of story.

But as time went on, the emotional pain began to fade, the grief lifted, and instead of focusing on what I had lost through my mistakes, I started to focus on what I had gained. As I navigated new territory, I started to see just how much I learned as well as the value of all these painful and hard lessons.

So here I go again. As I write this I am in the process of restarting my own business. I have matured quite a bit as the result of all that grief I went through the first time around. But I am still changing. And seeing all these changes has been one of the most rewarding experiences I have ever had. Even though a million textbooks could have told me how to avoid making the mistakes that have led to these changes, I am sure I would have gone ahead and made them anyhow. For better or worse, I am the live-and-learn type. And I am learning how to enjoy the learning as much as the living.

Believe me, if I can overcome my mistakes and losses, anyone can. No matter how bad your mistakes may feel at first, you can get over them and even learn to appreciate them if you:

- **Recognize when you're in denial.** As they say in those twelve-step programs, admitting you have a problem is the first step.
- **Curb your anger.** Anger can be productive and mobilizing but it needs to be kept in check. It is a normal and healthy part of living if you let it out constructively and move on from it as soon as you can.
- **Refuse to get stuck bargaining.** "Was I really wrong?"

"Should I confront the problem or sweep it under the rug?" "If this goes my way, I'll never make another mistake again and I promise I will . . ." There's no point in trying to bargain your way out of your mistakes. All actions have their consequences, and you're better off facing these immediately.

- **Problem-solve your way out of depression.** Whatever it is that you've lost, you can't help feeling sad when you think about what your mistake may have cost you. But turn your focus on how to fix the mistake and watch as your despair transforms into optimism.

- **Accept yourself as you are.** It's called "trial and error" for a reason. We all make mistakes and lots of them. The sooner you figure out that your mistakes don't define you any more than your successes, the sooner you'll be able to accept them as the crucial part of the learning process that they are.

I have to say that out of success and failure, I actually found failure a much more interesting and internally rewarding experience. And yes, very painful as well. But as much fun as you can have with success, it's easy. There's not the same challenge, not as much to learn, and not the same opportunity for emotional, spiritual, or intellectual growth. Failure, on the other hand, is a different story.

Now don't get me wrong. It's not as if news of my mistakes now fills me with joy. On the contrary. I still go through all the phases of grief I outlined in this chapter, just like anyone else. Except these days, I know that underneath all the pain, disappointment, and frustration that comes with making a mistake, great development is afoot. As one of the most effective triggers of change, mistakes and the grief they cause us can be a beginning. The beginning of a stronger *you*.

12

KEEP THE FLAME ALIVE

CANDLES AND FIRES are hazardous to my personality. I become so mesmerized by them that my conversation fades to a mumble as my eyes glaze over and I become totally fixated on the flame. But as I've found, you can't just sit and watch a fire expecting it to burn forever. You have to tend to it if you want it to last. The same is true of our passion for what we do—you'll have to stoke it to keep it alive.

Passion can get you much further than just hard work alone. But like fire, passion needs oxygen to stay aflame. In other words, to refuel your commitment and dedication, you need to go outside yourself for some fresh air. Too much time in our own heads, our own patterns, and our own comfort zones is a recipe for complacency. Outside of us, in other people, places, and worlds, there exists a wealth of incredible oxygenating material. The type that reminds us that no matter how much we have already seen and done, there is still so much left to aspire to and discover.

My Story

I adore bridges. If there is anything that fills me with a sense of the largess of life it is a big bridge. So while many people head for nature when they need refueling, I head straight for these large steel, concrete, wooden, or metal structures. I see bridges as monuments to connection and ingenuity. The desire we have to reach other places, explore, and connect across divides, and the intelligence that we can muster to figure out just how to do that. I am humbled by the stoic power of bridges and inspired by the majestic quality that the best examples possess. Just thinking of my favorites is enough to remind me that life is so much bigger than me and my goals. That life has been in motion before me and will continue without me. Bridges give me relief from the pressure that the world quite possibly revolves around my plans, a silly notion but one that can creep up on me if I am not careful.

One of my very favorite bridges happens to be in

my hometown. Melbourne's West Gate Bridge snakes and curves across the skyline, connecting a very industrial area to the inner city. Supported by massive concrete pylons from underneath, it slopes gently upward to a crescendo and then slopes down again with the same rhythm. I have driven over and back across that bridge whenever I needed to get out of my own head. Times both good and bad. When I was flush with success and my head felt like it was going to explode with shock, joy, and elation, I would take to the bridge and confront the vast expanses that life offers. I have also driven over that bridge in tears, when my world felt like it was crashing down around me, and I felt so sorry for myself and so scared of the future that a reminder of how much movement there is in the world was just what the doctor ordered.

I also drove over that bridge for no real reason at all. Perhaps I would be on my way to work and just needed to remember how exciting the everyday can be. Despite the ups and downs, running a lipstick company can get mundane at times, so it was extremely important to have something that helped me tap into my passion for appreciating life and giving it my best.

When I was little, I made up a pastime called "secret games" to keep me amused when I was bored. While the name may sound dubious, "secret games" was really just play-acting . . . me and my imagination acting out different plots and fantasies for my eyes only. I may be older, but I still have my "secret games"—except nowadays these are the strange little rituals, like driving back and forth across a bridge, that keep me inspired. Although these practices may sound childish, they are actually very important and very much the secret to keeping my passions alive.

TAP INTO YOUR PASSION

Seek out some spot, place, scene, or thing that gets you outside of yourself and connects you to something far larger. This can be something as grand as the Grand Canyon or as small as a personal memento, tchotchke, or souvenir. Like that tram car ticket I told you about at the end of the last chapter, reminders of earlier successes and turning points have the power not only to transport us back in time but to help us return to face the present with a renewed outlook. You'll be amazed how much something like this can help boost the driving force that initially fueled your goals.

LESSON 59: **Your customer is always right**

I used to love watching a TV show called *Kids Say the Darnd-est Things*. It focused on kids and some of the wonderful, often brutally frank things they say before socialization really kicks in to censor their conversation. Watching it, I would often laugh out loud as well as marvel at the profound ideas kids have about life. We always think that it is we who bear the responsibility of teaching them, but they teach us a lot too. While their fresh and unusual take on things may not be correct in the strict sense of the word, we can all profit from respecting their point of view. A point of view that is going to differ from your own.

Of course, kids aren't the only ones who can offer us this new and exciting vantage point. Customers can do the same thing. I define "customer" as anyone you rely on to buy, believe in, or benefit from a good, service, or job that you are doing. When all is said and done, these are the people whom we are here to serve. These are also the people who ultimately decide what we represent. In the chapter on marketing, I emphasized how important it is to communicate a message and stand for something. That is our part of the bargain and the part that is entirely within out control. What we have no say in, however, is how our customer interprets our message. And in the end, that is the only interpretation that truly matters.

As you become accustomed to success, keeping the customer at the forefront of your mind is a surefire way to stay passionate and innovative, as well as to ensure that you are putting your energy right where it always needs to be . . . with the people who make your success possible.

My Story

Have you ever met a skyscraper of a man? The type of man that exudes power, influence, and conquest? These types are usually tall, but they don't have to be. Sometimes it is all attitude that has this effect, an attitude of complete and utter leadership. In this case, the man I am thinking of happened to be about six foot three, lean, and in possession of blue eyes so piercing they could level you within a split second. He was the closest thing to God that we had in my industry and was treated as such. Just to walk a hall with him was to watch people hold their breath in awe and trepidation. Some people loved him, some hated him, but pretty much everyone admired him.

Despite the fact that he terrified the living daylights out of me, I both loved and admired him. In fact, we got along famously right from the start. It was one of those situations when someone scares you so much, you figure you may as well be yourself because they will be able to see through any show.

So I was myself with him, a very nervous version of myself but genuine nonetheless, and he liked me for that. In the scheme of this man's stature, abilities, and lifestyle, I was about as big as a speck on his perfectly tailored suit, so people (myself included) were amazed that he still treated me like I mattered. No one would ever have expected him to take time out of his Fortune 500 day and wander down to a department store to see me meeting and greeting customers at an in-store appearance. To put it in some perspective, it would be like Walt Disney himself (if he were still alive) wandering down to some obscure street corner to see a guy that someone at his company had hired to hand out flyers in a Pluto suit. Very unlikely.

The first thing that alerted me that something was going on was the strange pallor that came across the faces of my coworkers. I was elbow deep in lipstick swatches—sleeves rolled up, the undersides of my forearms covered with brightly colored stripes. Stick a feather in my hair and I would look like a tribal warrior decorated for battle. And that's just what retail is—a constant battle for the attention of customers.

With so many choices available, getting a customer's attention is a privilege. On that day I was keenly aware of this, so I was doing my best. I was also keenly aware that the air suddenly felt thicker and that all around me spines were straightening. I was helping a lady choose a lipstick and we were both standing over the display unit. I sensed something behind me and subtly looked over my shoulder to find the looming presence of this Master of the Universe. He was just standing there, paused. Now this guy had gotten to a point in his life where no one dared let him pause or hang loose. Secretaries, underlings, and entourages ensured that every second was accounted for.

I was about to do the same. Drop everything, turn around, and greet him immediately. But then it was my turn to pause. No, I decided, the customer comes first. I should complete the sale. So I went on serving this woman, heart pounding as if somebody with a walkie-talkie was about to wrestle me to the ground like an insurgent. He waited and waited, but this woman was very needy when it came to advice on her lipstick choices. I could feel him shifting from foot to foot, and each shift seemed to resound as loud as thunder in my nerves. He probably stood there for all of six minutes before finally giving up. As he was about to walk past me, I was afraid to meet his eyes for fear of narrow slits.

But somehow I managed to look up and meet his gaze, only to find a grin that stretched from ear to ear. I had handled it exactly the way he would have expected me to and he wouldn't have wanted me to do it any other way.

Your customer may not always be nice, appealing, funny, interesting, happy, pleasant, attentive, or even particularly sane, but they are always right. In order to absorb this I remind myself that in this context the word "right" is not about being factual or accurate, it is about being important. Each and every customer is of the utmost importance and their experience, feedback, and reactions are key to avoiding a complacency creep. The less complacent you are about your customer, the more passion you can maintain for what you do.

It comes down to curiosity. Being curious about what makes your customer tick, both in terms of what you are putting out there *and* how it is being perceived. Curiosity is the magic eraser of boredom. Going through what feels like the same experience for a long time is bound to bring about a case of the ho-hums. But take out your curiosity, sprinkle it over that experience, and poof, like magic it suddenly appears entirely different.

LESSON 60: **You're not alone**

Speaking of boredom, I don't actually get bored when I do such boring things as washing dishes, tidying up, scrubbing tiles, or doing laundry. I am far too perplexed to be bored—perplexed that I am doing this same activity again! I seem to have a built-in forgetter in the menial tasks department. I assume that if you have done them once you will never have to do them again. So every time my preposterous theory is proven wrong, I am taken aback ("You mean to say I have to do the ironing *again*?!"). This is what you call a "fool's paradise." My foolish notion that each time is the last time saves me from the horrible truth, that unless I become enormously wealthy, a hermit, a psychopath, or extremely unhygienic, I am going to do these tasks hundreds, even thousands of times again. A very discouraging thought.

It is hard to get motivated to do something that you know will need to be done over and over again. Like keeping others motivated. We already did that, right? Weren't these people sufficiently motivated a month ago? It's time to concentrate on something else, right? Wrong. Motivation is an extremely exhaustible resource, both in yourself and in others.

Keeping others excited about what they are doing can feel like a full-time job. But make no mistake, it is a crucial component of keeping and growing success. Hillary Clinton famously stated that "it takes a village to raise a child," and the same is true of long-term success: It is not something you can do on your own. You will always need others to help you, believe in you, and be motivated to do their part.

Our coworkers, regardless of their role, have exactly

the same right as we do to enjoy what they do, find it fulfilling, and have a sense of ownership. "Sense of ownership" is one of those buzz-type phrases that is often used and rarely explained. Partly because there is no one explanation that fits all individuals. What constitutes a sense of ownership for one person may be completely different for another. Of course, as always, there are some generalities. People need to feel they have some influence and impact on their role above and beyond execution, that their thoughts are respected as well as their labor. To be treated purely as labor is draining to motivation. How motivated can one be about something that lacks any capacity for personalization or dialogue?

Dialogue is such an important aspect of healthy and vibrant working relationships. Inherent in dialogue is the concept of thoughts flowing two ways. Thoughts going one way is what happens in lectures, speeches, and presentations, but treat a colleague or employee as if they are perpetually an audience rather than a participant and their desire to really give you their best is going to suffer. We all know how frustrating it can feel to be constantly spoken at, but never spoken with. There are times and places for conversation and dictation, but the best managers, employers, leaders, role models, mentors, and teachers are the ones that make a point of doing both.

My Story

"Just because." How many times did I say that on the playground when challenged? It is such an easy response. And although it may have backed off a few bullies when I was ten years old, it is not effective in the workplace, particularly if you are in a position (which all of us are in some way) of keeping others enthused and doing their job at their best. As the founder and boss of my own brand it was also a tempting response to those who worked with me, even my board at times! The other response that came to mind was the Nike slogan "Just do it."

I can remember resorting to this stance a great deal in the early days. I may not have said it quite as bluntly as Nike, but that was what I was thinking and people can pick up on that. Now that I have had much more experience both in being a boss and having bosses, I have realized that what you gain in expediency from that method you lose in motivation. The other people walk away deflated, rather than enthused to do their part.

As my role has always involved dealing with customers and dealing with coworkers, I have learned over the years that what gets the best results for both scenarios is not dissimilar.

Out there on counters and selling floors, I would

never say "Just because" to a customer in response to why I think she should wear a certain lipstick shade. I take the time to explain and garner her confidence in the decision. She not only walks away happy with why she has the lipstick but may have also learned some new information that helps her for next time and builds trust in my brand, and not just dollars. Same goes for others in my office. If I take the time to let people into my decision making process rather than just barking the decision at them, they not only understand and feel included but they also learn more about what goes on in decisions at different levels. And guess what . . . I learn too! I cannot tell you the number of times that by letting others into a process rather than just dictating it to them, how much better the results have been, and how motivating it is for them and me!

There is that saying, "Give a man (let's change it to 'person') a fish and they eat for a day, teach them how to fish and they eat for a year." Discuss don't dictate, and the long-term benefits are like a feast versus famine. There is enough motivation for everyone to be satisfied and happy with their role.

To keep others enthused, motivated, interested, and excited, something needs to be about them as well; it can't just be one-sided. Even something like entertainment, where people pay to sit and listen or watch, requires audience participation via engagement. And engagement happens when emotion is stimulated and not just muscle. Talk with people, talk to people, but try talking at them and they will check out of the results, theirs and yours.

LESSON 61: Ivory Tower Syndrome

There is a strong correlation between power and height. Not height as in how tall you are, but height as in how high off the ground your feet are. When you go to meet with a powerful person, chances are you will have to ride an elevator. You know someone is really powerful when they are on the highest floor. We often pay a premium for getting as far off the ground as possible. Air travel is expensive. Penthouses are expensive. And stilettos . . . boy, can those be expensive!

Success opens doors to ivory towers filled with the lofty thoughts, big ideas, and breathtaking views. This is part of the fun of being successful. But just because success grants you access to an ivory tower doesn't mean you have to develop a case of Ivory Tower syndrome.

Ivory Tower syndrome (ITS) can affect people once they have become used to their new position—and it is not as straightforward as arrogance or self-importance. In fact, I have seen people affected by ITS who are neither arrogant nor self-important. The symptoms of this syndrome are far more insidious and less obvious than that. They are as follows:

- Loss of perspective
- Inability to hear the word "no"
- Disconnection with the nerve endings
- Altered reality and blurred vision

While these symptoms are not contagious, the more they develop, the more the person affected by the virus tends to attract only those people who enable the virus to grow. Feeding off the denial of others, the virus systematically weeds out those who challenge it in favor of the company of the weak-willed and the "yes men." A case of ITS is very hazardous to your long-term success and can slowly dismantle everything you have worked so hard to achieve.

To counter ITS, you have to get back on the ground floor—that is, any area that puts you in direct contact with your end user, be that your customer or your employee, and reality in general. Ivory towers are built to help people get an aerial view of the playing field. These towers are often a necessary part of being able to dream, look far into the future, and articulate a vision. But for our brain to stay vital, it can't lose the connection to its nerve endings—we must come down from the tower every once in a while and step back out into the real world.

My Story

"Would you like to try Poppy lipsticks?"

I must have said this thousands of times in the early stages of my business. I spent innumerable hours standing in front of my little counter area in department stores, handing out Poppy brochures and being asked over and over again where the restrooms were. My favorites were those customers who would place their arms protectively over their face and cut a wide swath around me, no doubt anticipating a barrage of fragrance spray. If you ever need a crash course in coping with rejection, I highly suggest a stint as a promotional salesperson. My skin must have thickened at least an inch a week during this time. But I did learn how invaluable real frontline experience is and vowed that, come what may, I would never go too long without it.

The more well-known I became, the harder this was to pull off as people became self-conscious and censored themselves around me. But in those early days I got to hear everything, warts and all. Much to my shock and horror, I even heard that some of my customers were not using my lipsticks as God and I had intended (yes, we had a conference call on the subject). Instead of applying them in all their matte and opaque glory, some of my customers were finding that finish too heavy so they were lightening up the lipsticks themselves. The method they kept describing was: Dab on a little of the color, smooth it out over the lips so that it is almost see-through, and then apply a little Vaseline or gloss. The result was a sheer version of the same color, and sacrilege as far as I was concerned. But I soon realized that this was not an attack that had to be stopped but an opportunity for a whole new Poppy formula—a formula I would never have discovered had I not been working the counters for substantial periods of time.

To cater to the customer who loved my shades but wanted something with a little less punch, I went back to the labs and asked them to come up with a lipstick that delivered the same look as the process described above created. The result was lipstick called Poppy Sheer that utilized exactly the same names and colors but in a much lighter version. It was a big hit. I now had twice the options and double the customers!

The only problem now was explaining the difference between the two in simple terms. Handing out both Sheer and Matte Poppy brochures to customers rushing by at a mile a second, I needed a fast, effective way to get the message across. Eventually, I hit on one way both to stop customers in their tracks and explain the difference in the two textures in one fell swoop.

"Want to try the Coke and Diet Coke version of lipsticks?"

Worked every time.

Climbing the dream ladder and following goals requires a great deal of focus upward. But to stay abreast of developments in the market, don't forget to climb down from your new vantage point every now and again. Any position, even an elevated one, can become staid and boring once you become familiar with the surroundings and the perspective. You can even miss some major chances. For instance, from up high, a big opportunity may look like a tiny dot. But upon closer examination, what may seem like a speck could actually be a spectacular new idea or strategy to help you advance and keep you climbing those dreams with the same vigor you started with.

WHEN YES MEANS NO

The natural tendency to fall in love with our own ideas can be dangerous when we attain a position of authority. Once you achieve certain goals and prove your abilities, you may find that people are less likely to contradict or criticize your ideas due to any number of factors, such as their increased (often excessive) faith in your knowledge or an unwillingness to engage in confrontation or fear of losing their job. To prolong your success, you'll have to resist the temptation of building a "yes man" culture and encourage constructive criticism and debate by:

- **PRESENTING YOUR IDEAS WITHOUT BIAS.** Instead of saying, "I just had a great idea! How about we . . ." try putting it like this: "What do you think if we . . ."

- **ASKING FOR DISSENTING OPINIONS.** Go ahead and challenge the people around you to come up with the weaknesses of your idea as well as the strengths. If you find that others are struggling to come up with positives but have no shortage of negatives at their disposal, this could be one of the bad omens we talked about watching out for in chapter 10.

- **ASSIGN SOMEONE THE ROLE OF DEVIL'S ADVOCATE.** In meetings, people often prefer not to contradict their higher-ups. If you assign someone the role of devil's advocate, you are far more likely to stay grounded by hearing opinions that are not necessarily flattering.

Conclusion

It was the mail that finally did it. I had moved to New York City. I had finished my twelve years in my own company that I had started at eighteen years of age. I had left my friends, family, and my life as I knew it, and taken a job at a multinational corporation, my first since working in that lingerie store right out of high school. All this without shedding a tear, skipping a heartbeat, or increasing my pulse.

With all these changes taking place all at once, the adjustment was so drastic that I don't think I allowed myself to feel anything for the first few weeks. I didn't want to know what I was feeling—just in case it happened to be terror.

The reality of what I'd done dawned on me one cold December morning, when I set out to mail a thank-you note to my new boss, whose Christmas cocktail party I had attended. I had been in New York for about one month now, and to deal with what would turn out to be a brutal Northern Hemisphere winter, I had bought a heavy, down-filled SUV of a coat—bulky, rugged, ungainly, but extremely common. As I slipped it on to go out and mail my letter, I was not anticipating a difficult or momentous experience.

I knew exactly where I was going—directly to the

large green mailbox on my street corner. I had my envelope ready in my gloved hand, address, stamp, and zip code in order. But wait a second . . . where was the mail slot? The box had "U.S. Mail" embossed in big official letters and looked for all intents and purposes just like a regular mailbox. Except I couldn't find the mail slot to save my life. I looked all over. On the sides, at the top, underneath . . . nothing.

I felt very forlorn standing there in the snow, at a loss for what to do. That's when it hit me. I was no longer in my country of origin. I was no longer living in the same place I was born, the same place where I grew up, the same place where I knew how to do something as basic as mail a letter. Now I was here in New York. Everything was new now. I had to relearn things that I had known how to do ever since I was a kid. It suddenly occurred to me that I had made a major change. I walked back into my apartment in a completely different emotional state than the one I'd left in — and all just from what I had assumed would be a run-of-the-mill errand.

You should have seen me those last weeks in Melbourne. I went over absolutely everything to do with the move. I got what needed getting — my dental records, my medical records, copies of my birth certificate, and all the rest. I canceled what needed canceling — bank accounts, subscriptions, mail delivery. I sorted through everything, organizing and redistributing my things and papers into boxes and files I'd purchased just for the occasion. I went past my old school. I said good-bye to special places. Everything. By the time I was actually on the plane to New York, I thought I had prepared myself so well and so fully that I had it all covered. Nothing could surprise me. Least of all a damn mailbox.

But like I keep finding out, life is full of surprises. As we start out on the road to success we invite surprise; in fact, we hope for it. We look for where and how we may be pleasantly surprised, where we might find some luck, some fortuitous circumstances. But when we arrive at success, the tables can turn and the idea of surprise seems more like a threat than a thrill. We do all we can to minimize, manage, and master any surprises, often failing to remember the important function that unpredictability can serve in our lives — it can fan the flames of our passion for what we do.

Here are three key strategies for staying motivated and keeping the element of surprise in your professional life long after the novelty has worn off:

- **Tune in to your customers.** Be it a boss or a client, the people you want to serve are the final judges of how well you're doing your job. And boy, do they have a fresh perspective. Listen to their feedback because when it comes to your future success, your customer's perception counts above and beyond all others.

- **Relate to your team.** The people who are helping you on the road to success are more than just worker bees laboring away for your benefit. They are treasure troves of valuable and often unexpected information. Allow them to inform and inspire you every chance you get by remembering to speak *with* them as well as to them and avoid speaking at them.

- **Get your feet back on the ground.** The Ivory Tower syndrome can afflict even the most well-intentioned of us. You never know what effect success will have on you. So before you get to the top, make a vow to never forget where you came from by going back — often. The view from the top is majestic and may inspire you to dream of a bright future, but the view from the trenches is what will keep you in touch with what's going on today and help you deal with the present.

You can stay alert, engaged, and excited about your work by understanding that you can never prepare for everything. Just when you think you've got it all under control, just when you're feeling at your most invincible, something is bound to take you unawares. Green mailboxes that you thought were for sending mail are going to turn out to be storage boxes for use by postal employees. It is the blue boxes that are for the mail. But I couldn't have known that on that snowy Sunday, just as I couldn't have known that what was awaiting me just outside my door would be one of the most poignant moments of my life. And you don't know where, when, and how those moments are coming for you and who they come with. Meaningful moments are filled with surprises (and vice versa). Invite them in and you invite passion and long-term success as well.

EPILOGUE

THE LAST WORD
ON THE VERY BEGINNING

WELL HERE WE ARE. We have finished the book. Are we any wiser? Only to a certain extent because wisdom comes from experience, from your heart and soul, and not from the mind alone. What you have read in this book is how I gained some wisdom through my experiences. A wisdom that at times was painfully learned but always preciously processed. Yet despite all this wisdom, all these experiences, am I actually any wiser?

Yes and no. Yes, I am wiser about my experiences to date and about my past. As for the future, well, your guess is as good as mine. You see, I am once again about to launch headlong into the unknown. I am once again going to follow dreams, take risks, and give my ideas a go. All the wisdom in the world can only help me to better prepare; none of it can predict. So, yes, I am scared. I am worried, doubtful, anxious, insecure, and everything else that any human being feels when extending themselves.

But I am still willing.

I hope you are too. I hope you are willing to believe in yourself. To believe in the possible regardless of how probable it may be. To put yourself on the line and know that you too have what it takes to succeed.

There is no one determining factor, no guarantee, no variable, measurement, formula, magic, fact, or secret that you don't possess. There is no certainty when it comes to what makes success.

However, there is only one certain way to find out.

Just give it a try.

Everything and anything you can imagine begins from there.

Your Story

That's enough about me . . . now, it is your turn.

ACKNOWLEDGMENTS

I WOULD LIKE to acknowledge the following people, places and things

My two fabulous editors, Greer Hendricks and Leah Furman, who have shaped this into something I am proud of.

My caring agent Dan.

My friend Miranda who made me feel so good when she said to me "You are a machine!" every time I told her how much I had written.

My other close friends past and present who put up with me.

My mother (now there's a book!).

A towering and inspiring icon of the cosmetics industry (you know who you are).

Cara Castiglione, Cynthia Sparks, and Arnold Joseph who mean more to me than they know.

All the receptionists over the years who have put my calls through.

My little apartment in New York where I sat for six months and experienced the joy and privilege that is writing.

Mr. Bear . . . the teddy bear I read the text to during the process . . . such a great listener!

And most important: I would like to acknowledge every single woman who has ever bought, worn, or considered my lipsticks. Without you . . . none of this would have happened.

Vanessa Manel

Made in the USA
San Bernardino, CA
19 December 2015